Classical Guitar Method
Volume One

By Bradford Werner
wernerguitareditions.com
thisisclassicalguitar.com
2017 Edition

WERNER GUITAR EDITIONS

Classical Guitar Method - Volume One

by Bradford Werner

2017 Edition

Distributed by
wernerguitareditions.com
thisisclassicalguitar.com

© Bradford C. Werner 2017
All Rights Reserved.

Sharing Info

This work is licensed under the Creative Commons Attribution-NonCommercial-NoDerivatives 4.0 International License. View a copy of this license: http://creativecommons.org/licenses/by-nc-nd/4.0/
> You can share this work but must give credit and link to my site. You may not sell this work, use it for commercial purposes, alter it and/or distribute a modified version.

Printing the PDF

This PDF has been designed for double sided printing. Place it in a three ring binder with dividers for each section. Binders are great as you can easily supplement it with extra materials of interest to the student and/or teacher. You are *not* permitted to print and *sell* this book.

Hard Copies

Physical print editions of this book are available at: thisisclassicalguitar.com or wernerguitaredions.com

Special Thanks

Uroš Barič, Michael Dias, Erin Fisher, Brett Gunther, Natasha Pashchenko, and Adrian Verdejo.

Contents

Part I - Progressive Method

8	Brief definitions of music notation
11	Reference for Basic First Position Notes
12	Open String Pieces: Etude No. 1 & 2, Nocturne Duet
16	Third String Notes, Moderato, A Fairy Tale Duet
19	First and Second String Notes, Five Melodies, Ode to Joy Duet, Dynamics, Etude No. 3
27	Third String Review, Twinkle Twinkle Little Star, Etude No. 4, Jazz Cat Duet
31	Melodies and Duets: Au clair de la lune, Oh Susana, Waltz Duet by Czerny, Minuet by Wilton Duet, Morning Duet by Diabelli
36	Open Bass Strings, Etudes No. 5, 6, and 7
40	Fourth and Fifth String Notes, Etude No. 8, C Major Scale, Note Review
44	Eighth Notes, Minuet Duet by Hook, Etude No. 9, Vsi so venci Vejli, Flow Gently, Sweet Afton Duet
50	Two Voice Textures, Etude No. 10 and 11, Dotted Quartet Notes, Little Birch Tree in the Field, The Skye Boat Song
56	Fifth String Notes, Note Review, Capriccio Duet by Logy
60	Sixth String Notes, Note Review, Note Naming, Leyenda Theme by Albeniz,
64	Accidentals, Chromatic Scale, Greensleeves, Minuet in G Duet by Petzold
68	Tutu Maramba, Django Swing, Etude 12 - à la Brouwer, Minuet Duet by Krieger
72	Sor Study No. 1 Op. 60, Siciliano by Carcassi, Übungen by Mertz, Etude13 - Farewell

Part II - Strumming & Fingerstyle Accompaniment

76	Strumming: Hey Ho, Frère Jacques, London Bridge, Amazing Grace, Red River Valley, Tom Dooley, Danny Boy, Shenandoah, Scarborough Fair
86	Fingerstyle: Scarborough Fair, Will the Circle Be Unbroken, Saint James Infirmary, House of the Rising Sun
90	Pentatonic Minor & Blues Scales, Twelve Bar Blues, The Shuffle, Rhythm Riff Blues,

Part III - Technique & Warm-Up Exercises

94	Right Hand Technique Exercises No. 1-10
96	Left Hand Technique Exercises No. 1-3, Single String Chromatic Scales
100	Beginner Scales: E Chromatic, C Major, G Major, F Major, A Minor, E Minor, D, Minor

About this book
This book teaches classical and fingerstyle guitar skills with a focus on the rich pedagogical tradition of classical guitar. Most learning objectives are covered through pieces and duets rather than exercises or descriptions. This allows students to perform full pieces from the first lesson. Working with a qualified teacher as well as watching the lesson videos should provide students with a healthy start to guitar. More specific information, theory, and exercises are learned in Volume Two.

How to use this book
Part I should be studied in progressive order, mastering every piece on every page. Incorporate Part II and Part III at any time, even the first lesson. Take lessons with a qualified teacher and watch the free video lessons to ensure you learn proper technique, musicality, and listening skills.

What will the student learn?
- How to play melodies in solos and duets
- Melodies with open string bass accompaniment
- Basic arpeggio pieces and patterns
- Reading music in first position (without key signatures)
- Basic chord strumming and fingerstyle accompaniment

What is left out?
This book omits information that might 'clutter up' the beginner learning experience. Music should be learned through listening and experience. Only a very small amount of theory and musical expression have been included. I encourage students to explore these topics with their teacher during weekly lessons. Some advice on theory and expression have been included in the free lesson videos which is a better medium for communicating musical ideas. After completing this book a more in-depth study of theory and musical ideas can be found in my Volume Two method book.

Free video lessons for this method
Video lessons have been made for this book to supplement the learning experience. Ideas about musicality and technique are discussed and demonstrated. Other ideas covered are tuning, rest and free stroke, and more. Find the lessons here: thisisclassicalguitar.com/lessons/

Volume Two method book
Students must complete Volume Two of this series in order to learn more in-depth musical concepts. Volume Two includes: new repertoire; new techniques; key signatures, scales, new time signatures; theory, musicality, rhythm training; new chords and accompaniment styles.

Rest stroke or free stroke? Nails?

Teachers have different opinions about the use of rest and free strokes for beginners. I have seen good results from both approaches. My beginner students use only free stroke until proper hand positions and a relaxed legato playing style are established. Students need not introduce right hand nails until hand positions and posture are firmly established. I would introduce nails during Volume Two.

Use of the left hand pinky finger

Students should use the left hand pinky for D and G (3rd fret of the first and second strings). This fingering is required for solo pieces later and also helps align the left hand. Students will have no trouble using the pinky if it is curved and in the proper position.

Memory and technique exercises

Beginner students, especially youth, do not need to be overly concerned with technique exercises. Motivation and inspiration should come from experiencing music for the first time through playing repertoire. Students should memorize their pieces and look at their hands while they play. However, a brief five minute warm-up with technique exercises can be beneficial to establish certain technical concepts. I recommend mastering all the right hand technique exercises first.

Great companion books for this method

- **Sight Reading For the Classical Guitar, Level I-III by Robert Benedict** - Sight reading with emphasis on interpretation, phrasing, form, and more: http://amzn.to/2o8bE0P
- **Celebrate Theory (Preparatory)**: Graded theory & musicianship from the RCM Toronto: http://amzn.to/2qgpHyJ

Tuning the guitar

Students should buy a clip-on tuner, I like the D'Addario Micro Tuner: http://amzn.to/2pecdpN
Tuning by ear should begin during the first lesson and relative tuning should also be taught:

1. Play the 6th string at the 5th fret and tune the open 5th string to the same pitch.
2. Play the 5th string at the 5th fret to tune the open 4th string.
3. Play the 4th string at the 5th fret to tune the open 3rd string.
4. Play the 3rd string at the 4th fret to tune the open 2nd string.
5. Play the 2nd string at the 5th fret to tune the open 1st string.

Follow the me for free lessons, sheet music, and pro videos

- Free and premium sheet music & tab: wernerguitareditions.com
- Free video lessons and instructional articles: thisisclassicalguitar.com/lessons/
- Email Newsletter: I send out a weekly email newsletter filled with lessons, sheet music, pro videos and more. You can sign up at the website or at: http://eepurl.com/hGOak

Getting Started - Finger Names

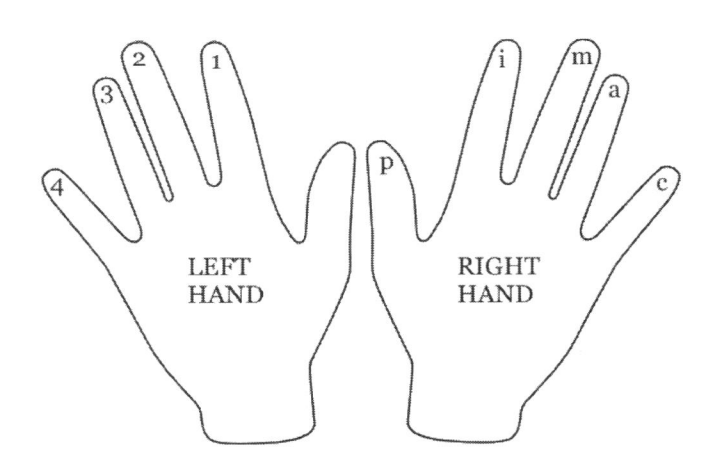

Left Hand Finger Names
1 = index
2 = middle
3 = annular
4 = pinky

Right Hand Finger Names
p = thumb
i = index
m = middle
a = annular (ring)
c = chiquita

Anatomy of the Classical Guitar

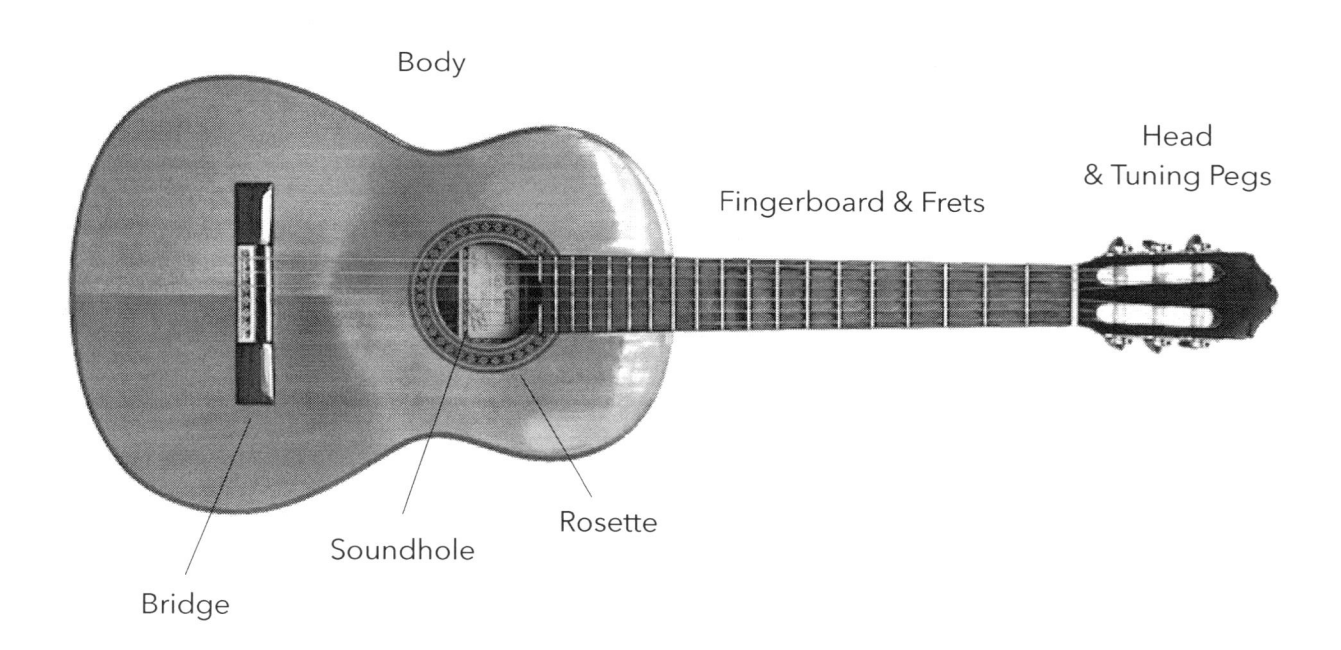

Body
Head & Tuning Pegs
Fingerboard & Frets
Rosette
Soundhole
Bridge

Image use - By User: Martin Möller (File:Classical Guitar two views.jpg) [CC BY-SA 2.0 de (http://creativecommons.org/licenses/by-sa/2.0/de/deed.en)], via Wikimedia Commons

Hand and Sitting Positions for Classical Guitar

Visit the archive of high res photos and video lessons including topics such as posture, left hand position, right hand position, and beginner tips: **thisisclassicalguitar.com/lessons/**

Sitting Position
- The head of the guitar is at eye level (guitar is at a 45° angle)
- Face of guitar straight up and down (not angled back)
- Sit up straight and relax the shoulders and neck

Right Arm & Hand
- Right forearm rests on the guitar in front of the elbow
- Right wrist is straight with a relaxed arch
- Right hand plays around the rosette
- Right hand fingers move into the palm, not up and away
- Right hand thumb is in front of the fingers

Left Arm & Hand
- Left hand thumb is vertical and behind 2nd finger
- Left palm and knuckles are parallel with the strings
- Left wrist is straight, not over-extended
- Left hand fingers are curved and on fingertips
- Left hand fingers play very close to the frets

Head of guitar at eye level (guitar at 45° angle)

Same position applies to guitar supports

Beat, Tempo, Notes

The **beat,** also called **pulse**, is the basic unit of time in a piece of music. For example, if you listen to a song and begin to tap your foot at regular intervals you are likely tapping 'the beat'.

The word **tempo** is used to describe the how fast or slow the beats are moving.

Notes are symbols used in music to represent the pitch and rhythm of a standard musical sound. **Pitch** refers to how high or low a note sounds.

Anatomy of a note:

● ○ Noteheads

♩ ♩ Noteheads with stems

♪ Stems with flags

Notes will be placed on a staff (5 lines), as shown below.

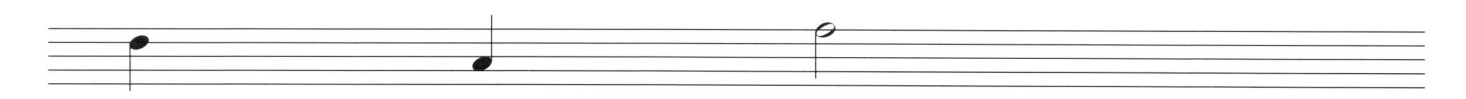

© Bradford Werner 2017, Victoria, BC, Canada
Free & Premium Sheet Music & Tab: wernerguitareditions.com
Lessons, Pro Video, & Blog: thisisclassicalguitar.com

Basic Musical Symbols

The **Staff** has five lines.

The **Treble Clef Sign** is used in guitar notation (also called the G Clef).

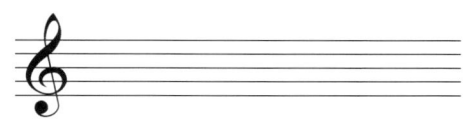

A treble clef with an 8 below is often used in guitar notation.
Guitar sounds one octave below where it's written.

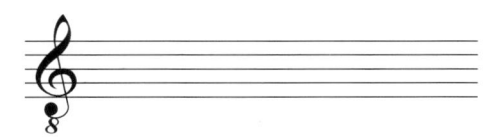

Bars, also called **Measures,** are used to divide the staff into sections.

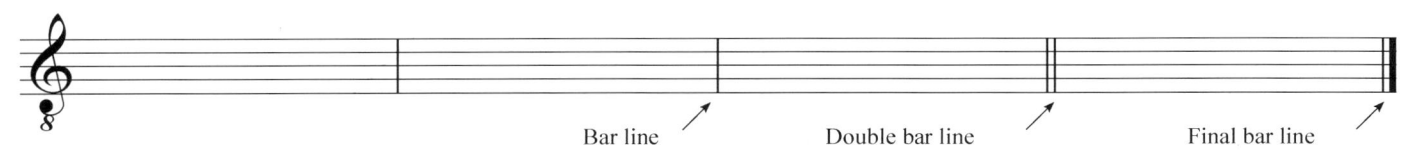

Bar line   Double bar line   Final bar line

The **Time Signature** tells you how many beats there are in each bar and what type of note equals one beat. To start, you only need to know about the top number.

The top number states how many beats are in each bar.
The bottom number states the rhythmic value of each beat.

Standard music notation starting on the lowest note of the guitar.
The lines above and below the staff are called **Ledger Lines**.

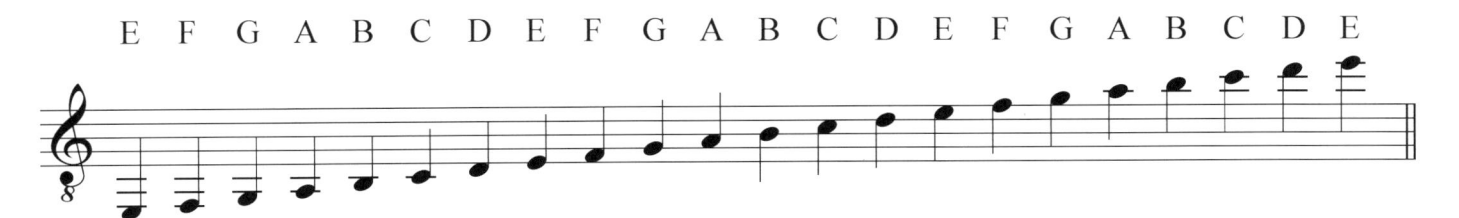

E F G A B C D E F G A B C D E F G A B C D E

© Bradford Werner 2017, Victoria, BC, Canada
Free & Premium Sheet Music & Tab: wernerguitareditions.com
Lessons, Pro Video, & Blog: thisisclassicalguitar.com

Notes & Rhythms

Line Notes Memorization: **E**very **G**ood **B**ear **D**eserves **F**ish.
Space Notes Memorization: **FACE**

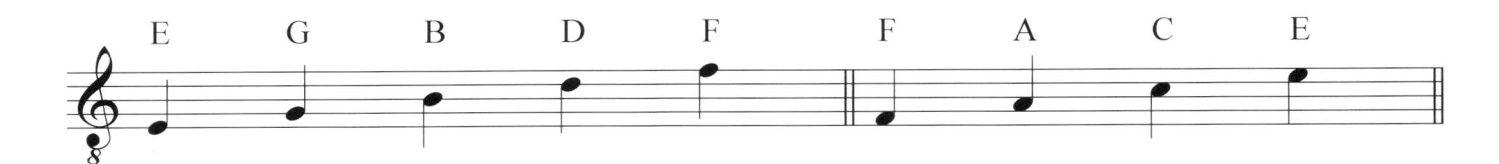

E G B D F   F A C E

The note names go up in the order of the musical alphabet.

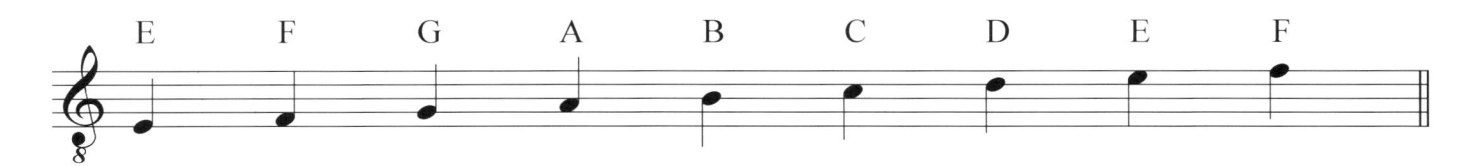

E F G A B C D E F

Rhythm & Beat Values

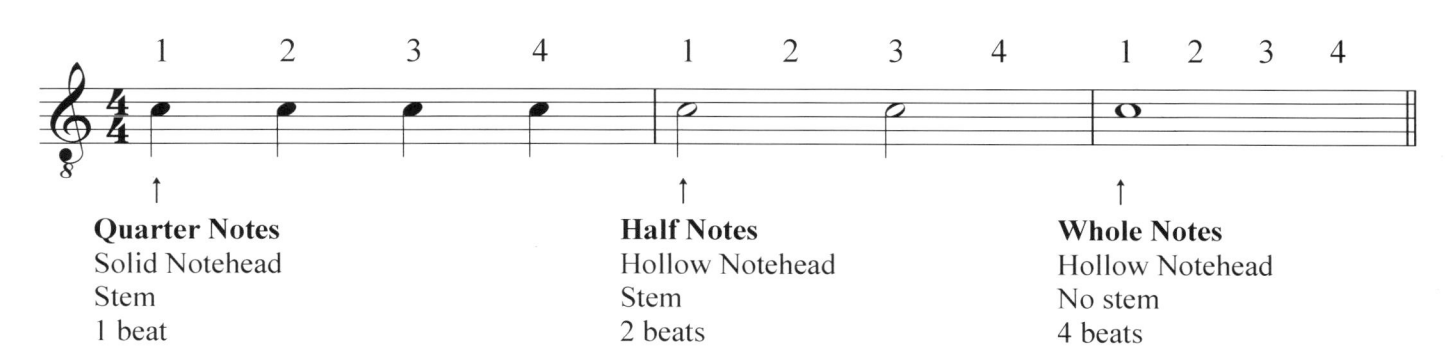

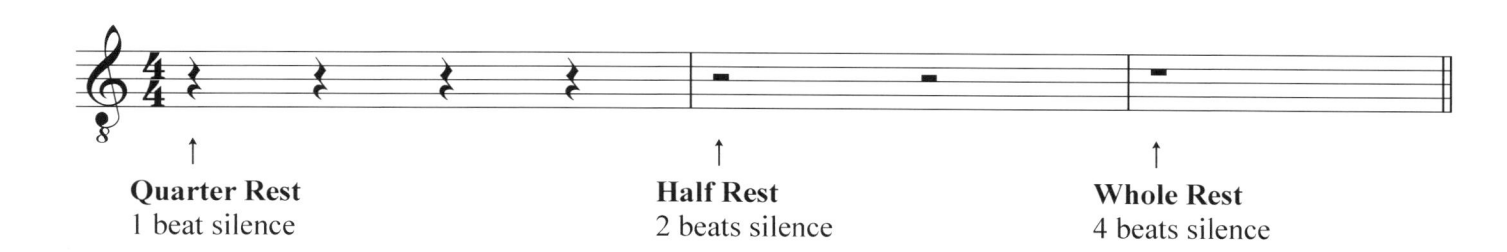

1 2 3 4   1 2 3 4   1 2 3 4

Quarter Notes
Solid Notehead
Stem
1 beat

Half Notes
Hollow Notehead
Stem
2 beats

Whole Notes
Hollow Notehead
No stem
4 beats

Quarter Rest
1 beat silence

Half Rest
2 beats silence

Whole Rest
4 beats silence

© **Bradford Werner 2017**, Victoria, BC, Canada
Free & Premium Sheet Music & Tab: wernerguitareditions.com
Lessons, Pro Video, & Blog: thisisclassicalguitar.com

Reference for Basic First Position Notes

You do not need to learn these notes yet.

Tag this page and mark the notes you learn as you progress through the book.
I suggest the teacher colour each new note with a yellow highlighter as you learn.
You should review all your current notes at the start of each practice session.

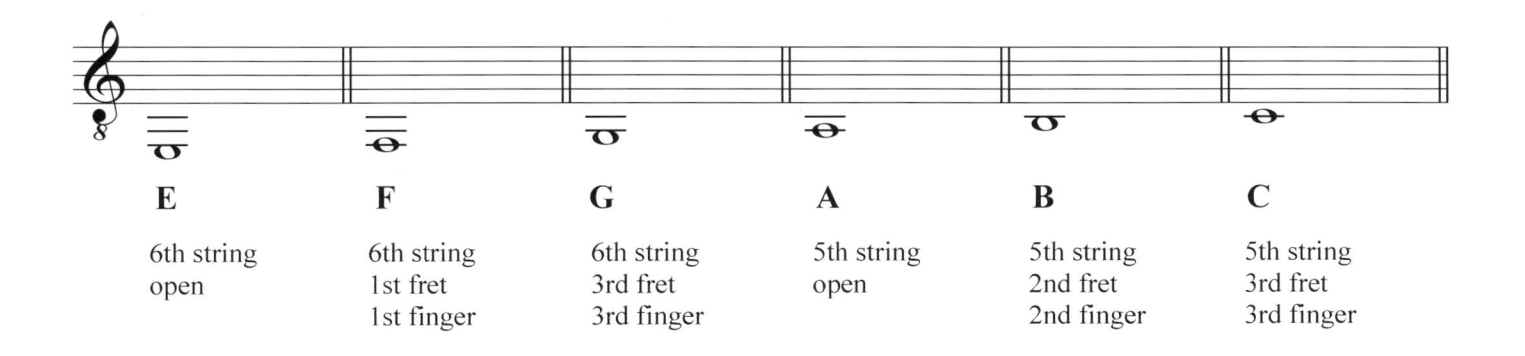

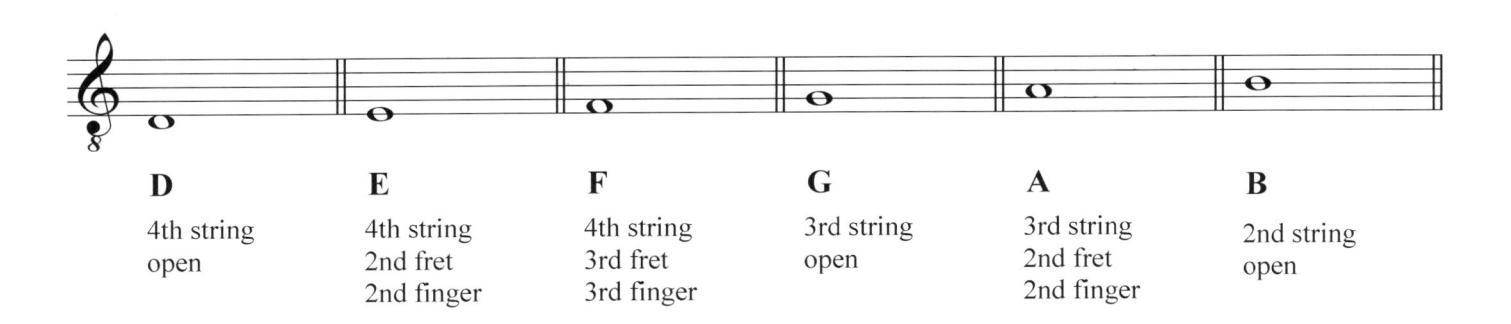

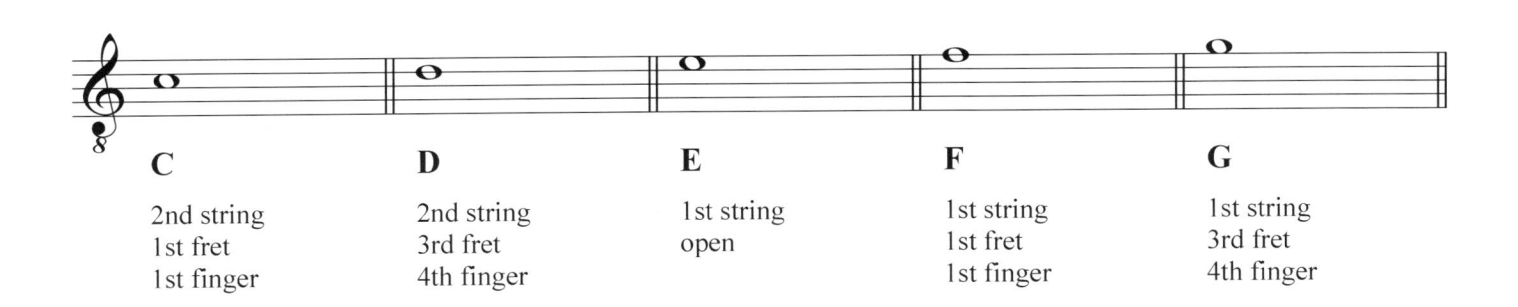

E
6th string
open

F
6th string
1st fret
1st finger

G
6th string
3rd fret
3rd finger

A
5th string
open

B
5th string
2nd fret
2nd finger

C
5th string
3rd fret
3rd finger

D
4th string
open

E
4th string
2nd fret
2nd finger

F
4th string
3rd fret
3rd finger

G
3rd string
open

A
3rd string
2nd fret
2nd finger

B
2nd string
open

C
2nd string
1st fret
1st finger

D
2nd string
3rd fret
4th finger

E
1st string
open

F
1st string
1st fret
1st finger

G
1st string
3rd fret
4th finger

© Bradford Werner 2017, Victoria, BC, Canada
Free & Premium Sheet Music & Tab: wernerguitareditions.com
Lessons, Pro Video, & Blog: thisisclassicalguitar.com

Notes for Etude No. 1 & 2

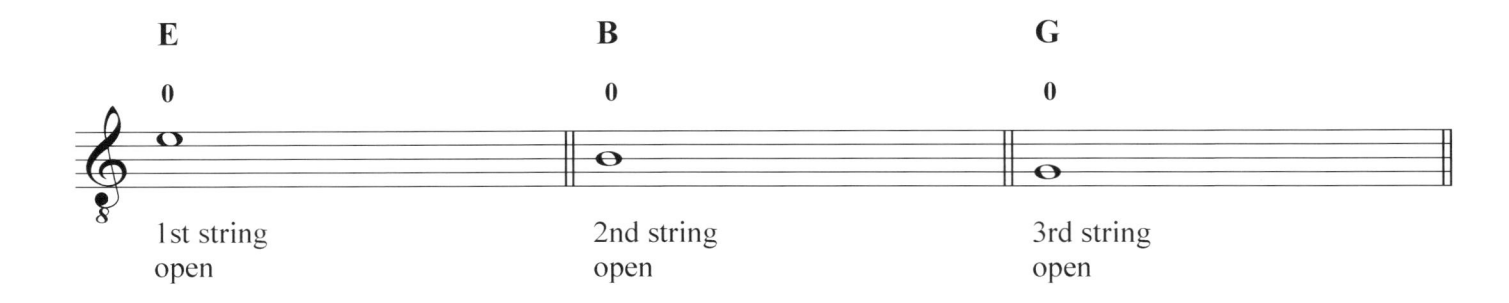

E   B   G
0   0   0

1st string open   2nd string open   3rd string open

Complete the following note names and string numbers

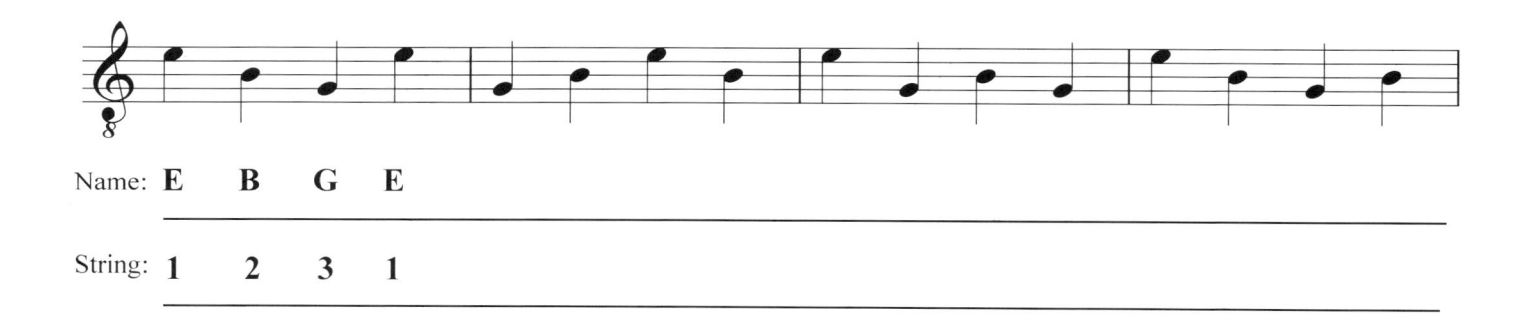

Name: **E**   **B**   **G**   **E**

String: **1**   **2**   **3**   **1**

Name: **E**   **B**

String: **1**   **2**

© Bradford Werner 2017, Victoria, BC, Canada
Free & Premium Sheet Music & Tab: wernerguitareditions.com
Lessons, Pro Video, & Blog: thisisclassicalguitar.com

Etude No. 1 - Melody

Ways to practice
Name the notes without playing
Count the beat while playing from start to finish
Say the right hand fingering as you play

Tip: Rest your right hand thumb on a bass string
to anchor the hand and minimize movement.

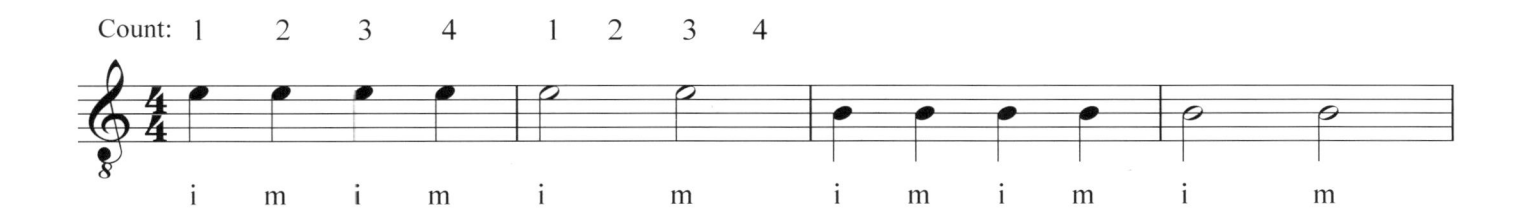

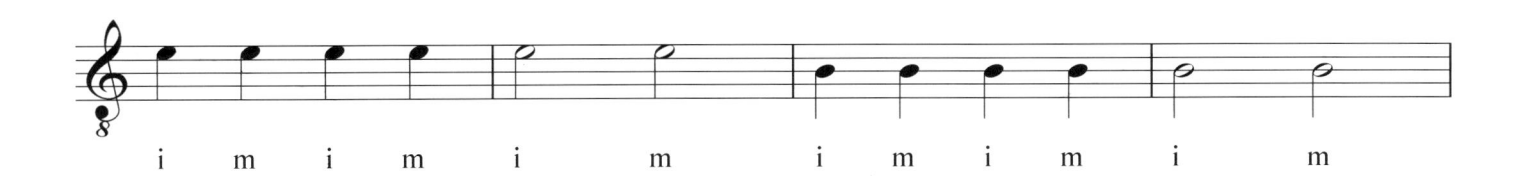

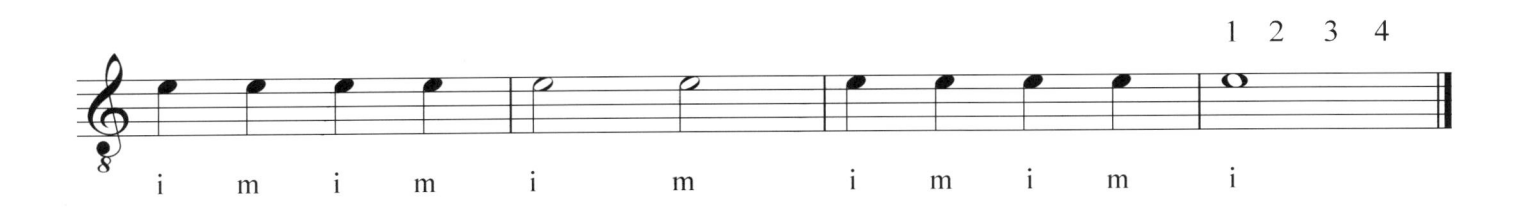

Etude No. 2 - Arpeggios

Arpeggios are notes of a chord played in succession.
Let all notes sustain (ring) and count out loud.
Keep the thumb in front of the fingers at all times.
rit. = *Ritardando* indicating a slowing down of the tempo.

Slowly

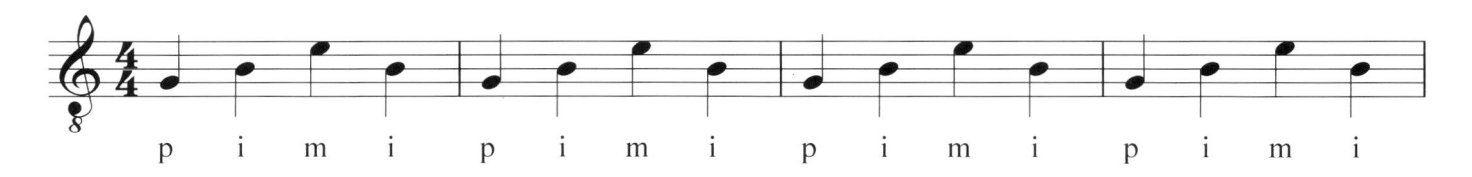

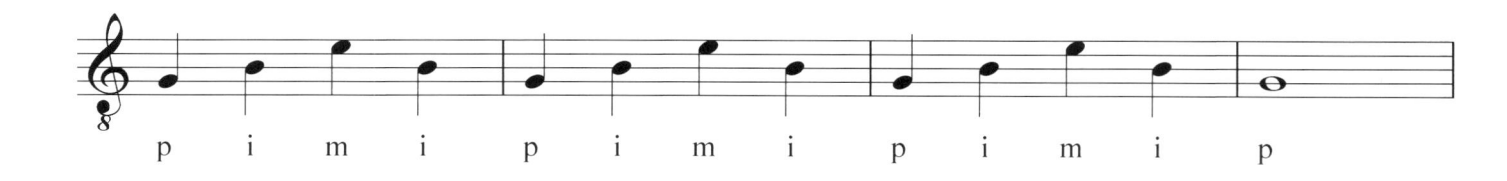

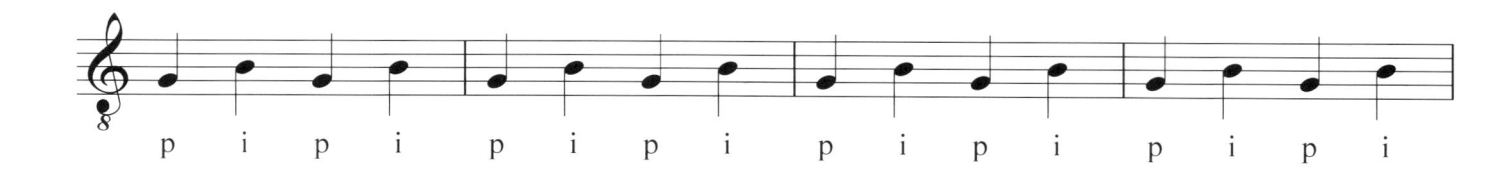

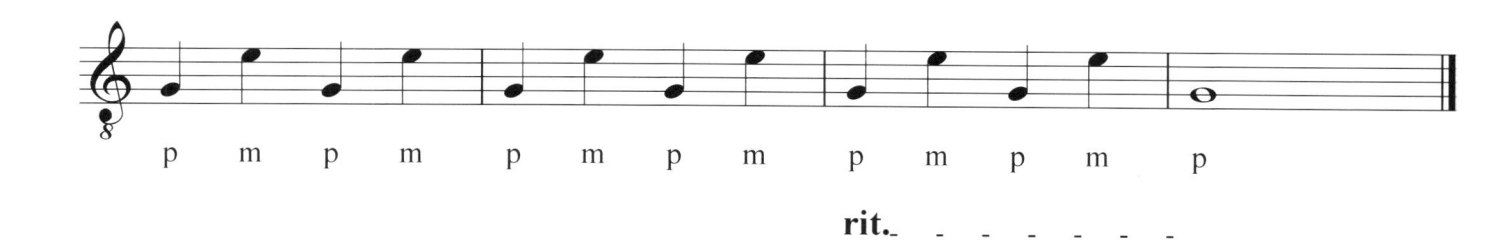

Nocturne (Duet)

The student plays the top part while counting out loud.
Stop the sound during bars containing rests.
Both lines have repeats. Repeat signs have dots facing inward,
therefore, the second line is repeated from bar 5.

Notes on the Third String

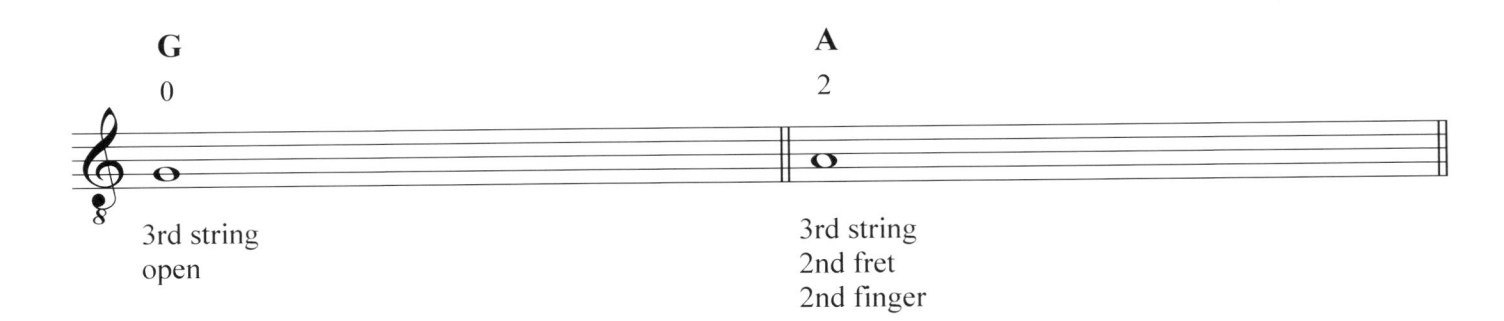

G 0
3rd string
open

A 2
3rd string
2nd fret
2nd finger

Complete the following note names, frets, and strings

Name: **G A**

Fret: **0 2**

String: **3 3**

Name: **A B**

Fret: **2 0**

String: **3 2**

Moderato Maple
(First Left Hand Song)

Say the note names out loud as you play. Moderato indicates a moderate tempo.
Keep left hand fingers curved, play on fingertips very close to the fret.
Playing close to the fret will stop buzzing and allow for a light touch.
'Anchor' the right hand thumb on a bass string.

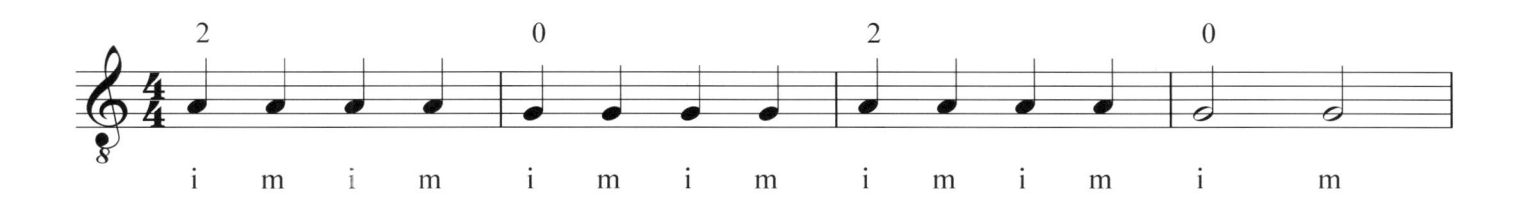

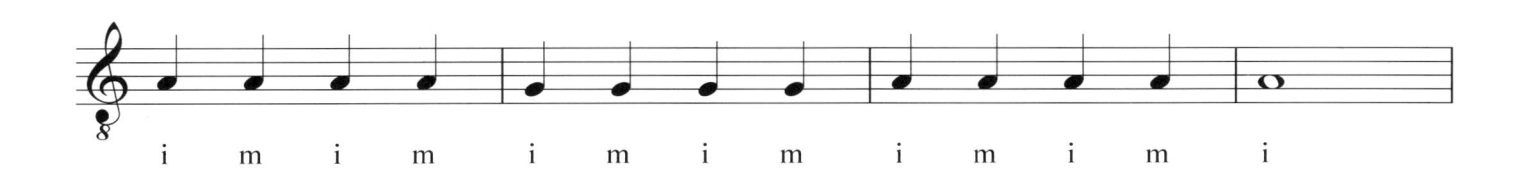

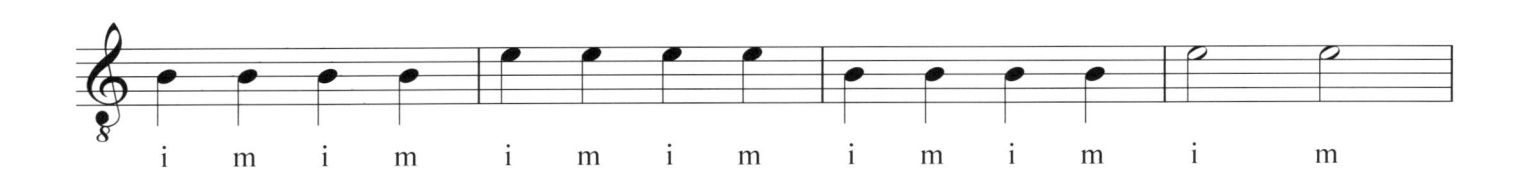

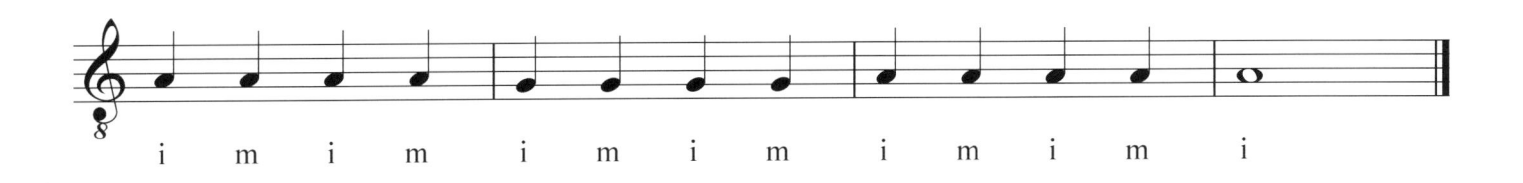

A Fairy Tale

The student plays the top part. Notice this piece has 3 beats per bar.
The teacher should arpeggiate (strum) the chords.

Notes on the First & Second Strings

The following notes use a similar pattern: open string, 1st fret, 3rd fret. Use the 4th finger on D and G as solo pieces will require it and it helps with left hand alignment.

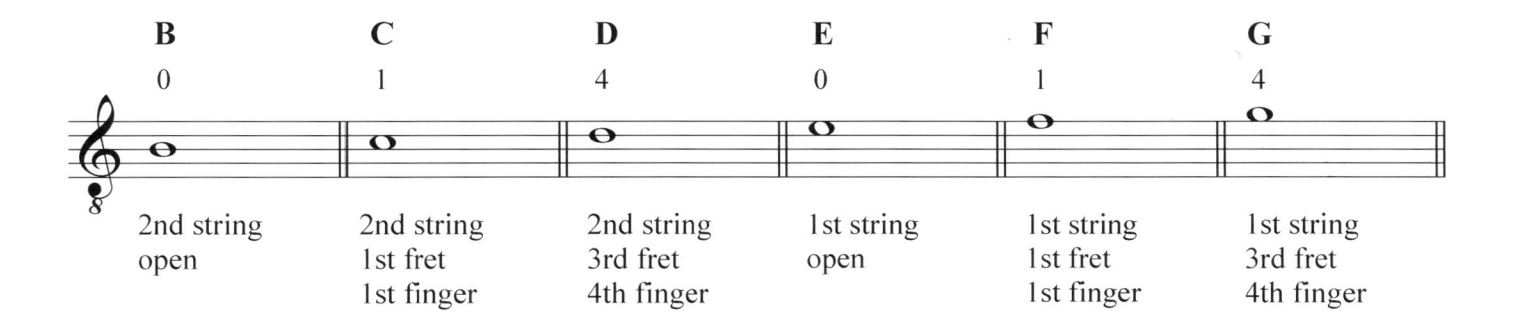

B	C	D	E	F	G
0	1	4	0	1	4

2nd string
open

2nd string
1st fret
1st finger

2nd string
3rd fret
4th finger

1st string
open

1st string
1st fret
1st finger

1st string
3rd fret
4th finger

Complete the following note names, frets, and strings

Name: **D C**

Fret: **3 1**

String: **2 2**

Name: **G F**

Fret: **3 1**

String: **1 1**

© Bradford Werner 2017, Victoria, BC, Canada
Free & Premium Sheet Music & Tab: wernerguitareditions.com
Lessons, Pro Video, & Blog: thisisclassicalguitar.com

Note Finder

Name: **B**   **C**

Fret: **0**   **1**

String: **2**   **2**

Name:

Fret:

String:

Name:

Fret:

String:

© Bradford Werner 2017, Victoria, BC, Canada
Free & Premium Sheet Music & Tab: wernerguitareditions.com
Lessons, Pro Video, & Blog: thisisclassicalguitar.com

Left Hand Practice

Say the note names out loud as you play the following exercises.
Keep left hand fingers curved, play on fingertips very close to the fret.
Playing close to the fret will stop buzzing and allow for a light touch.
'Anchor' the right hand thumb on a bass string.

Second String Notes

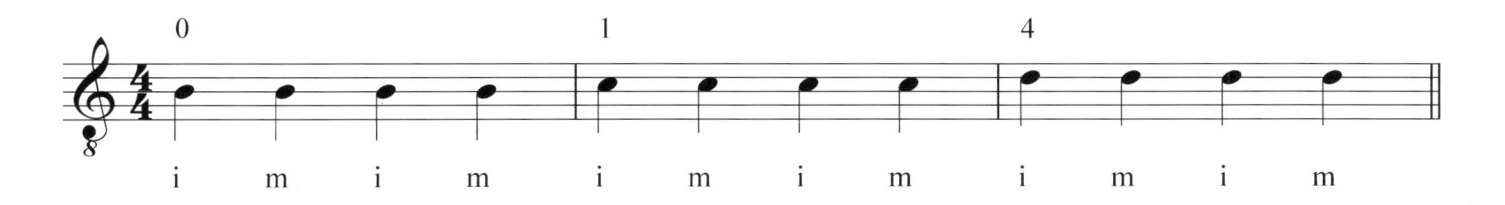

First String Notes

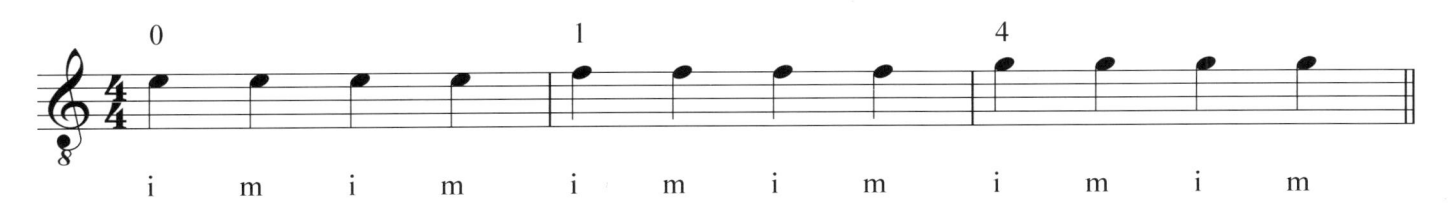

Both Strings Without Fingering

Five Melodies

Say the note names out loud as you play.
'Anchor' the right hand thumb on a bass string.

The Mountain

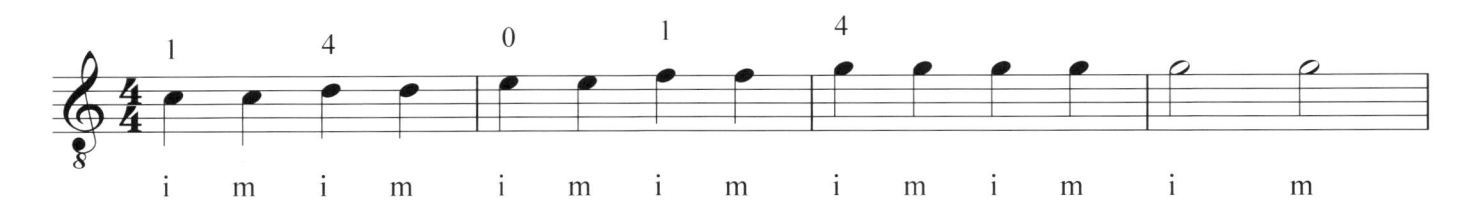

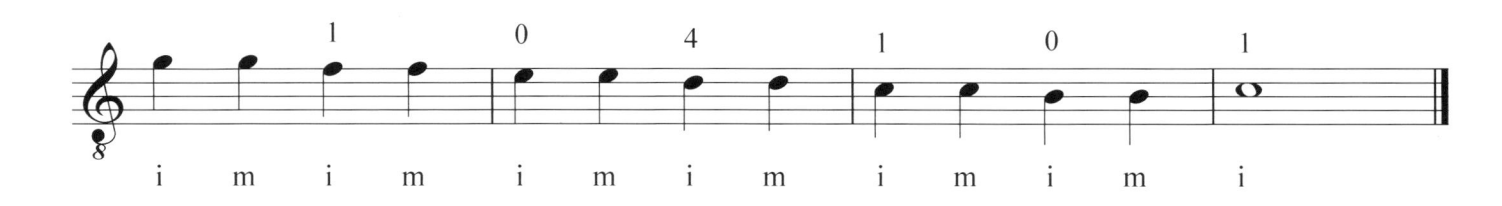

Theme by Joseph Haydn (1732-1809)

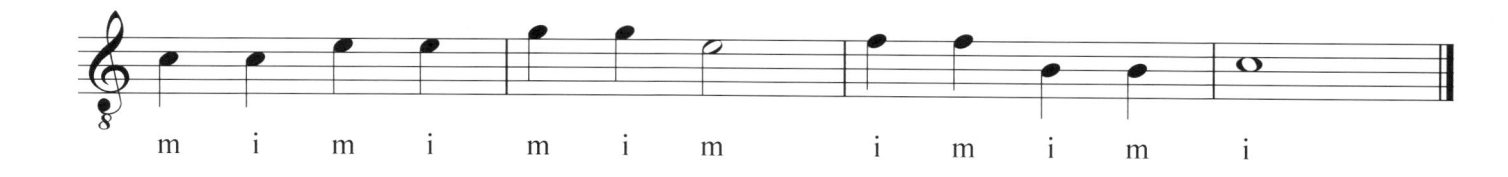

© Bradford Werner 2017, Victoria, BC, Canada
Free & Premium Sheet Music & Tab: wernerguitareditions.com
Lessons, Pro Video, & Blog: thisisclassicalguitar.com

Lightly Row

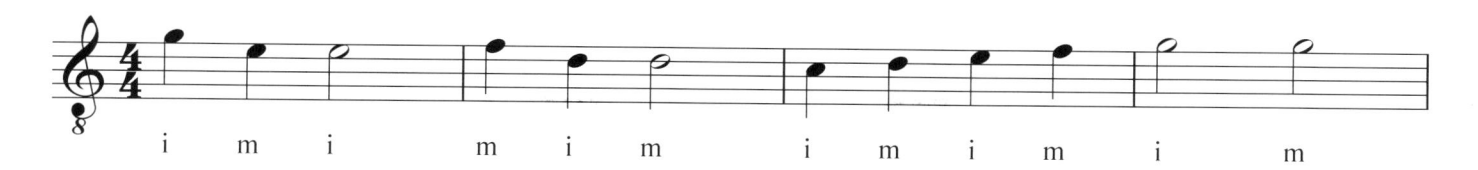

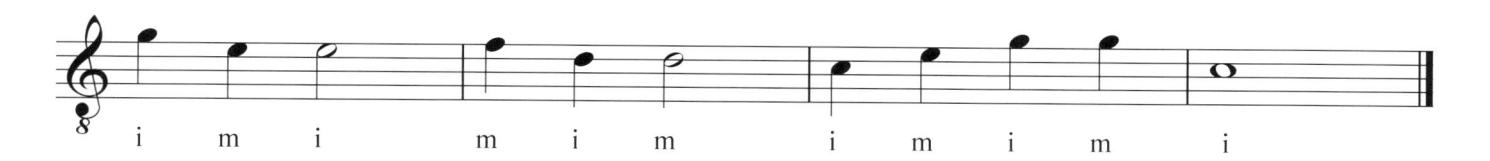

Go Tell Aunt Rhody

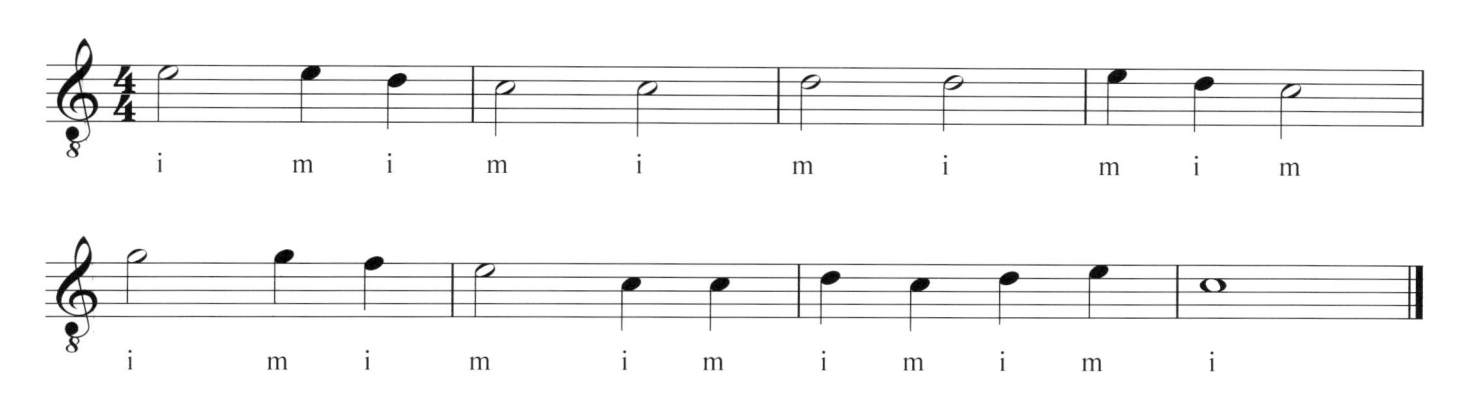

The Fox

This cunning little piece encourages proper left hand technique through listening skills.
Let all notes sustain by keeping C and D down while you play the open E string.
You will have to stay on your fingertips and curve your fingers to avoid muting the 1st string!

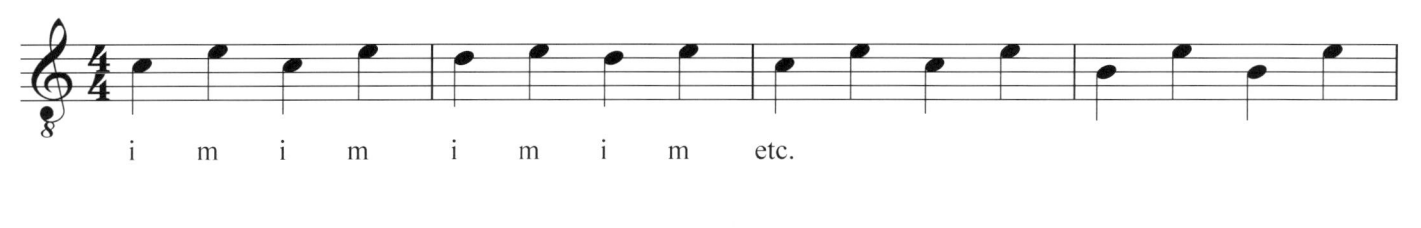

Ode to Joy

Ludwig van Beethoven
(1770-1827)

The student plays the top part with alternating i, m fingers.
Both parts contain the melody to help develop phrasing and rhythm.

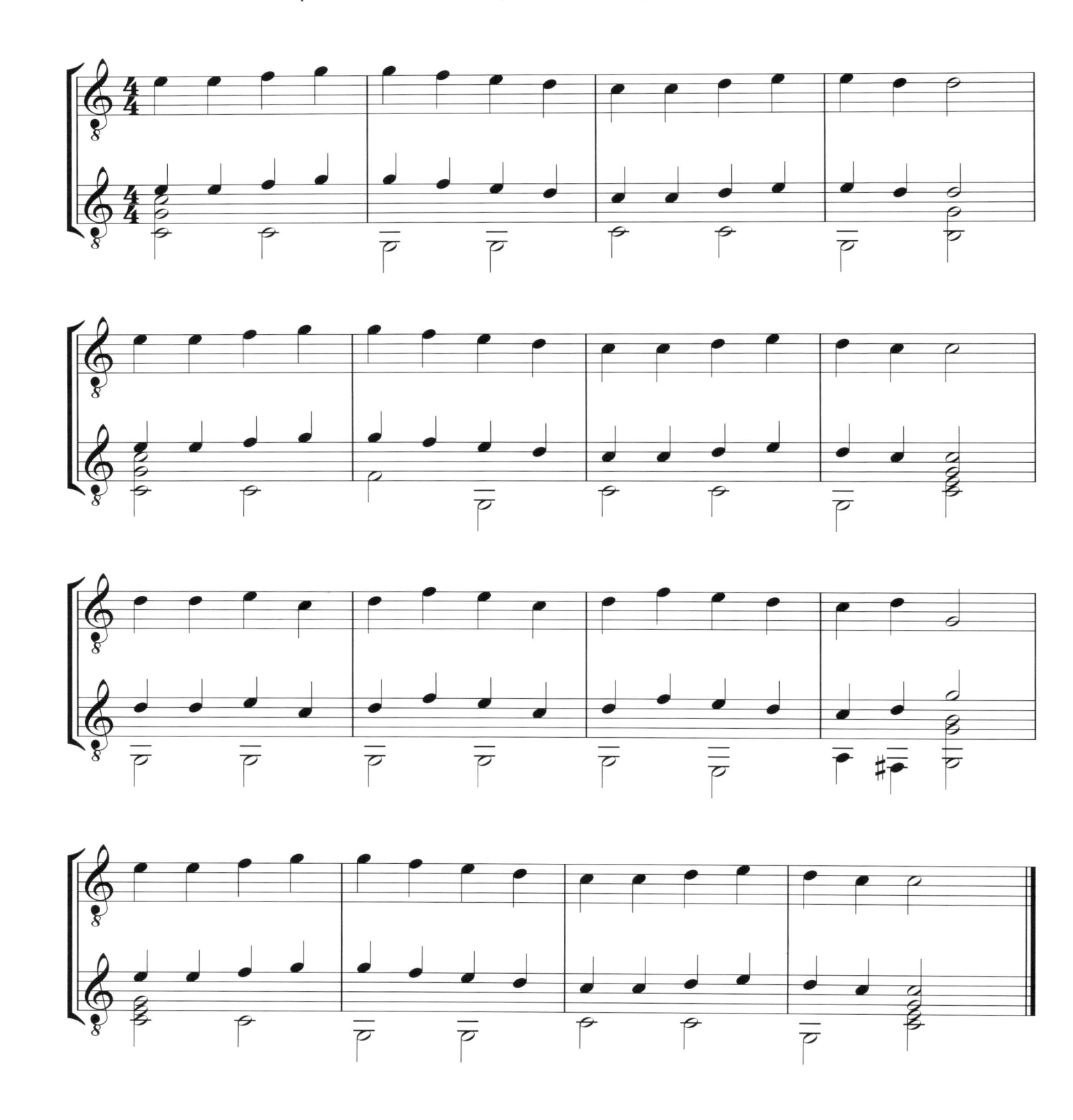

© Bradford Werner 2017, Victoria, BC, Canada
Free & Premium Sheet Music & Tab: wernerguitareditions.com
Lessons, Pro Video, & Blog: thisisclassicalguitar.com

Dynamics

Dynamics indicate changes in volume and can bring any melody to life. Dynamics are not always marked on the page but musicians add them for expressive effect. Here are a few examples of dynamics you might see:

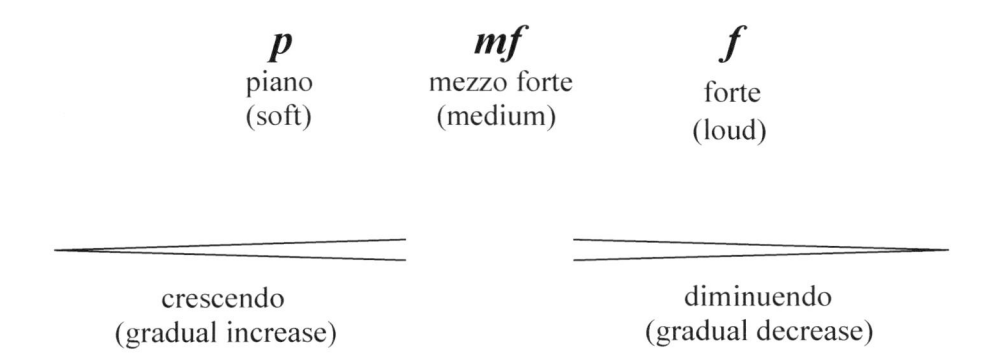

p
piano
(soft)

mf
mezzo forte
(medium)

f
forte
(loud)

crescendo
(gradual increase)

diminuendo
(gradual decrease)

Play the following example of crescendo and diminuendo

Play the following example of an echo effect (loud first line, soft second line)

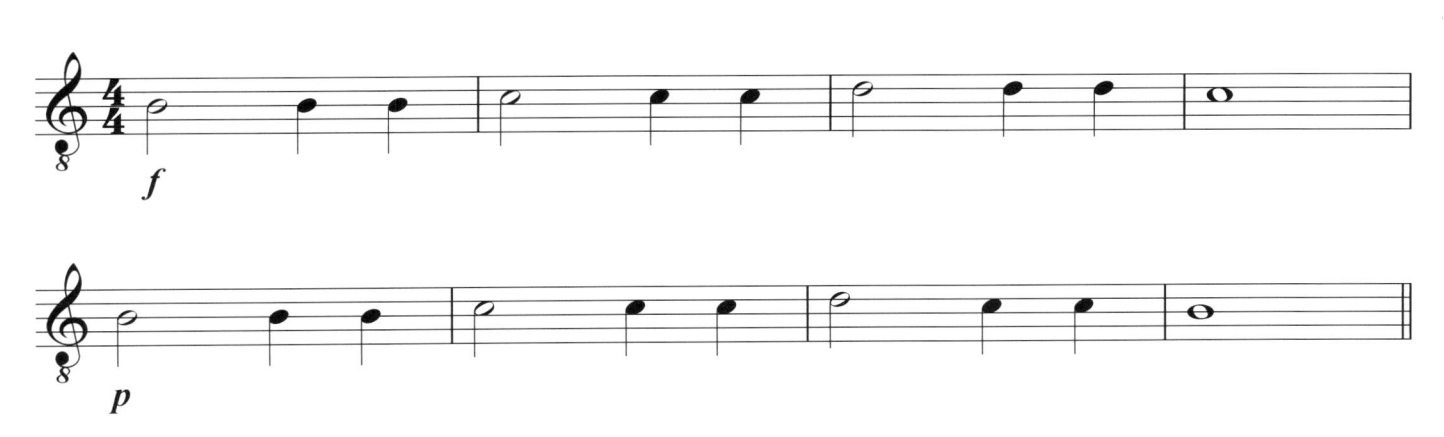

Etude No. 3 - Sound Picture

Remember: the right hand thumb plays in front of the fingers.
The last chord is strummed from the 3rd string with the thumb.
Follow the dynamics very carefully.

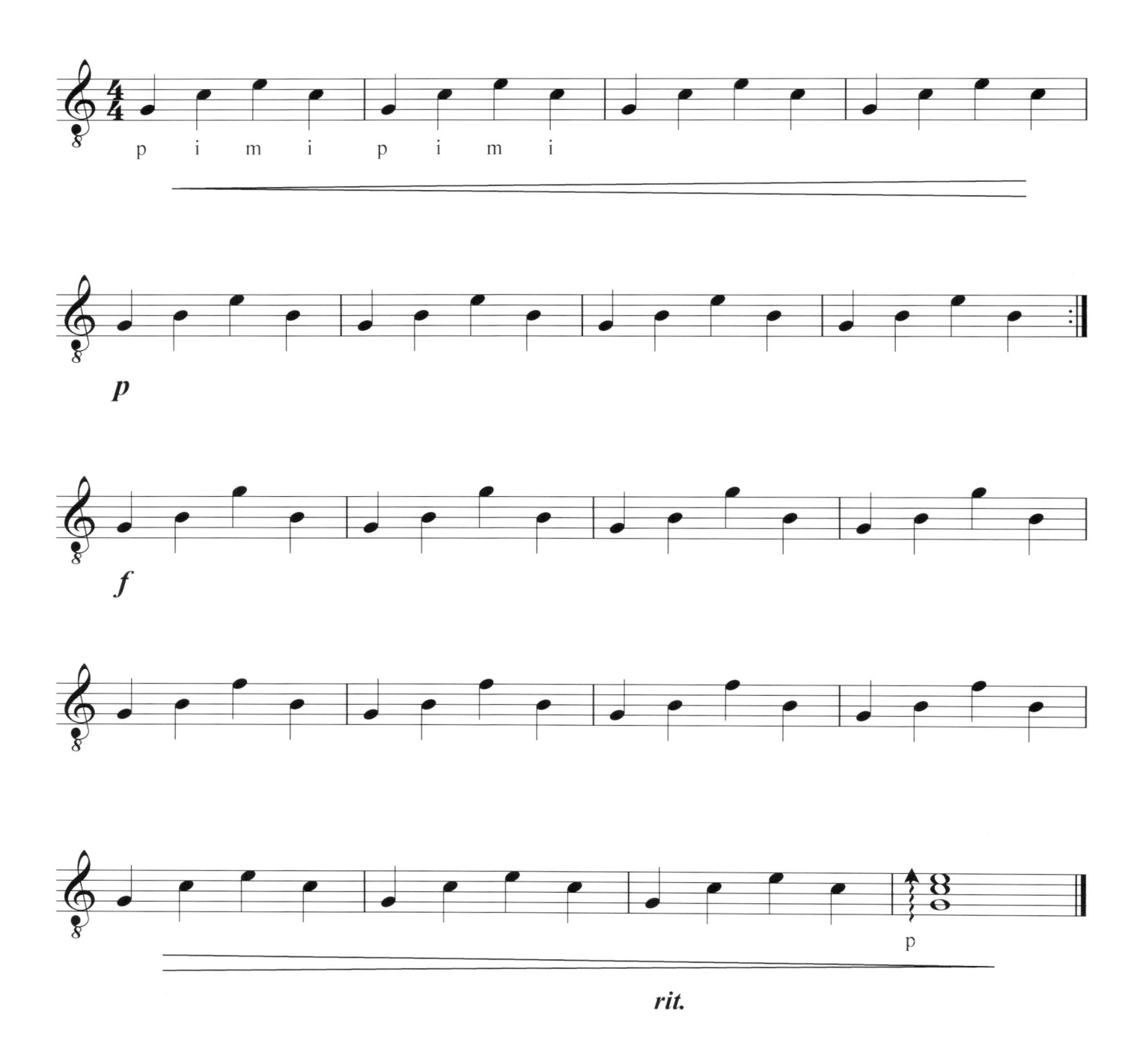

Review: Third String

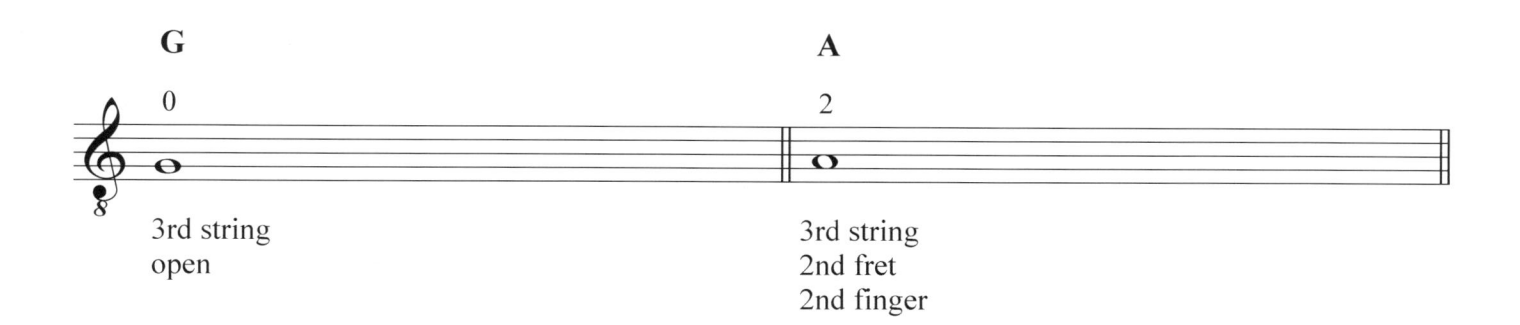

G — 0 — 3rd string, open

A — 2 — 3rd string, 2nd fret, 2nd finger

Name the following notes

Name:	G	A	B
Fret:	0	2	0
String:	3	3	2

Name:	G	E
Fret:	3	0
String:	1	1

© Bradford Werner 2017, Victoria, BC, Canada
Free & Premium Sheet Music & Tab: wernerguitareditions.com
Lessons, Pro Video, & Blog: thisisclassicalguitar.com

Twinkle, Twinkle, Little Star

Phrasing tip: sing the words as you play and imitate your voice.
Avoid emphasizing each syllable/note equally.

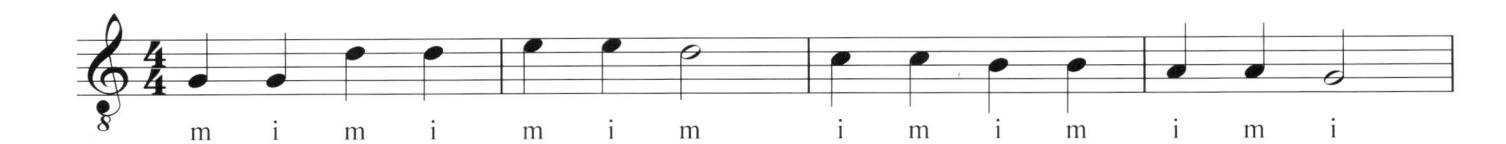

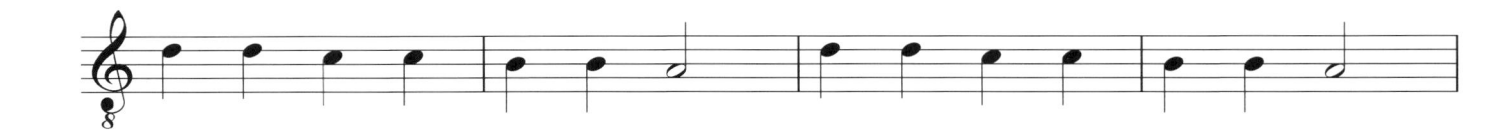

m i m i m i m   i m i m i m i m i

Lyrics
Twinkle, twinkle, little star,
How I wonder what you are.
Up above the world so high,
Like a diamond in the sky.
Twinkle, twinkle, little star,
How I wonder what you are.

© Bradford Werner 2017, Victoria, BC, Canada
Free & Premium Sheet Music & Tab: wernerguitareditions.com
Lessons, Pro Video, & Blog: thisisclassicalguitar.com

Etude No. 4 - The Birds

Hold down all the notes within each bar and let sustain.
Notice the time signature indicates only three beats per bar.

p   i   m   p   i   m

mf

p

f

mf   *rit.*

Fermata (hold longer)

© Bradford Werner 2017, Victoria, BC, Canada
Free & Premium Sheet Music & Tab: wernerguitareditions.com
Lessons, Pro Video, & Blog: thisisclassicalguitar.com

Jazz Cat

The student reads the notes and ignores the written chords.
Remember to use alternating i, m fingers.
The teacher plays the chords (leave out the 7ths if needed).
Accompaniment can be strummed or fingerstyle.
Vary the accompaniment pattern to encouarge musical flexibilty.

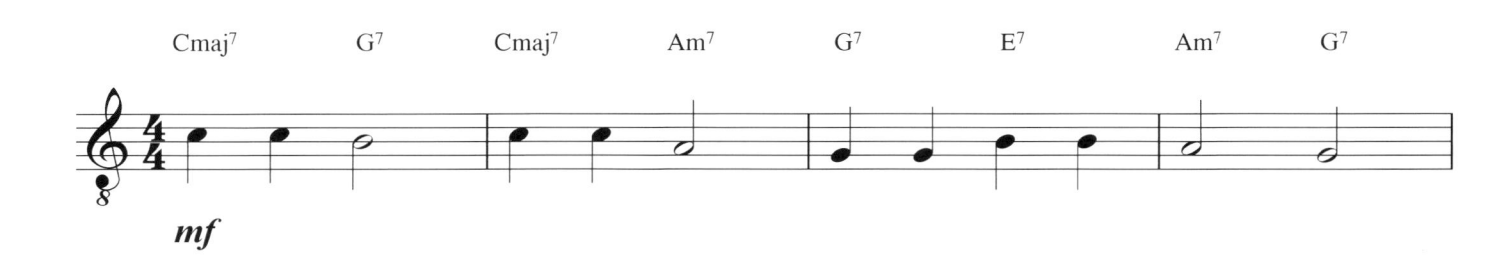

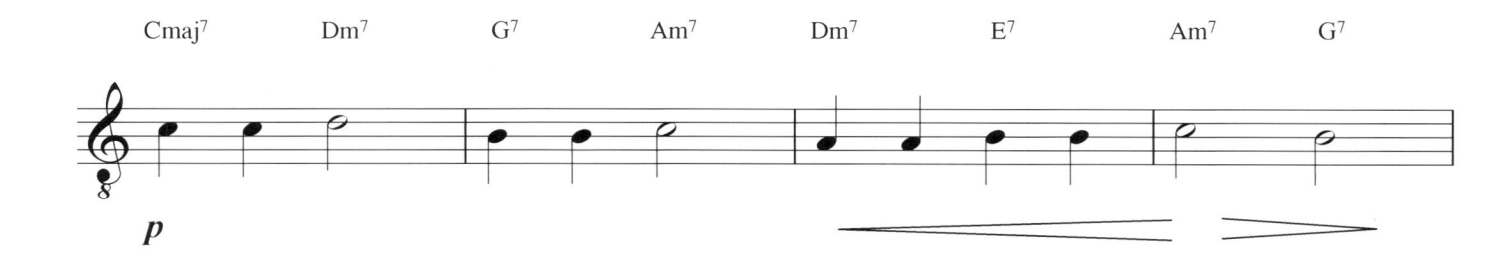

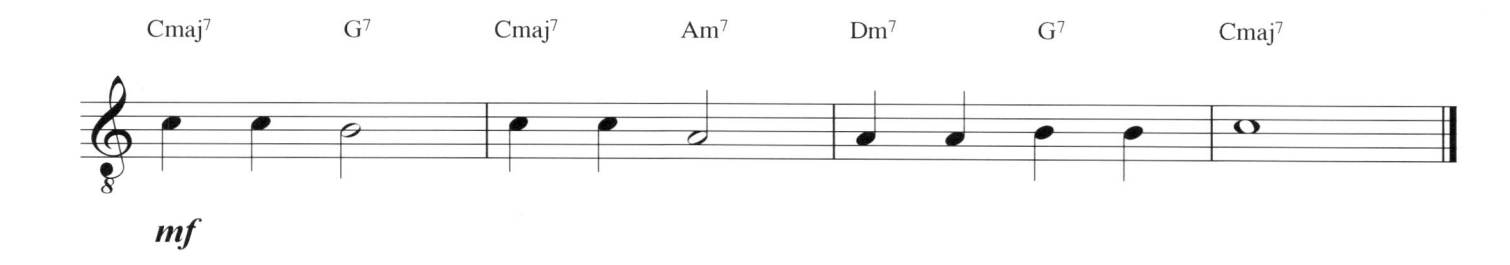

© **Bradford Werner 2017**, Victoria, BC, Canada
Free & Premium Sheet Music & Tab: wernerguitareditions.com
Lessons, Pro Video, & Blog: thisisclassicalguitar.com

More Melodies & Duets

The student plays the notes (ignore the letters indicating chords).
Remember to use alternating i, m fingers.
The teacher accompanies with chords (strumming and fingerstyle).
Vary the accompaniment pattern to encouarge musical flexibilty.

Au clair de la lune

Oh! Susanna

Stephen Foster
(1826–1864)

The student plays the notes. The teacher accompanies with chords.
Feel the beat mainly on beat 1 and 3 (cut time will be discussed in Volume Two).

Pickup Notes: A note that doesn't start on the first beat.
Count the missing beats in the pickup bar.

Dotted Half Note: The note near the end of the first line counts for 3 beats.

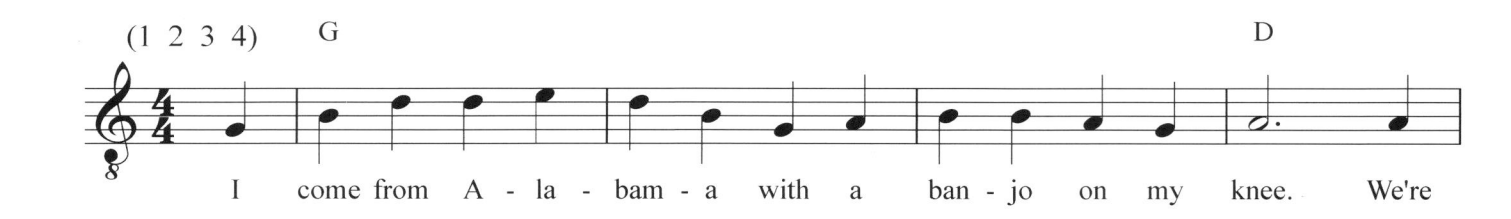

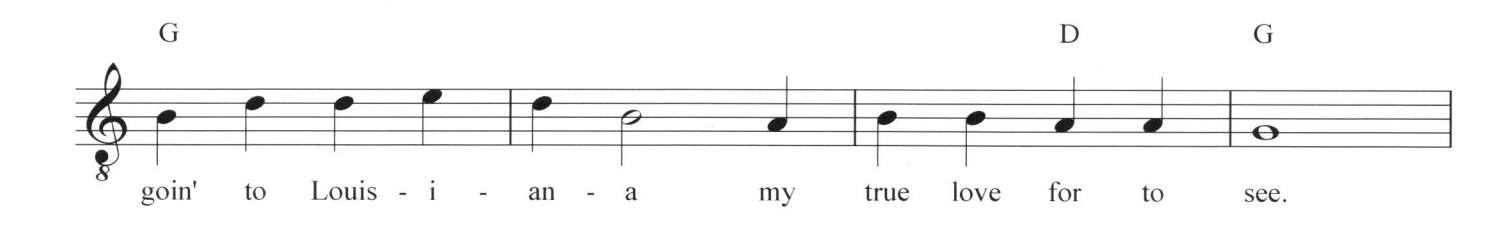

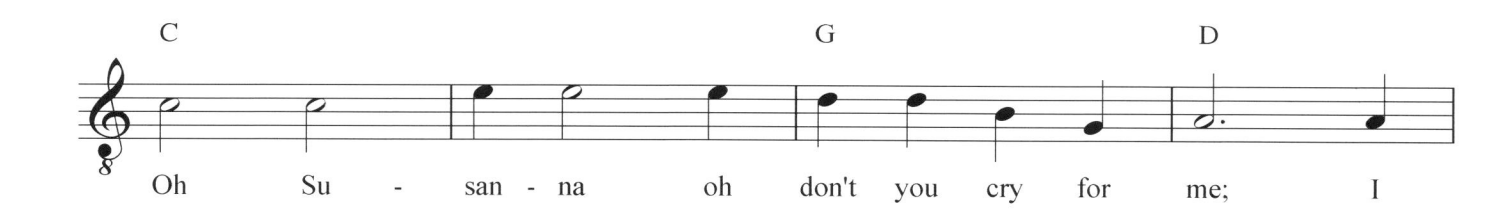

I come from Alabama with a banjo on my knee. We're goin' to Louisiana my true love for to see. Oh Susanna oh don't you cry for me; I come from Alabama with my banjo on my knee.

© Bradford Werner 2017, Victoria, BC, Canada
Free & Premium Sheet Music & Tab: wernerguitareditions.com
Lessons, Pro Video, & Blog: thisisclassicalguitar.com

Waltz

Carl Czerny
(1791-1857)

The student plays the top part. Notice the dynamics and *phrase marks* indicating *legato*: a smooth and connected sound from note to note. The dots above some notes indicate *staccato*: short and disconnected (opposite of legato).

Andantino

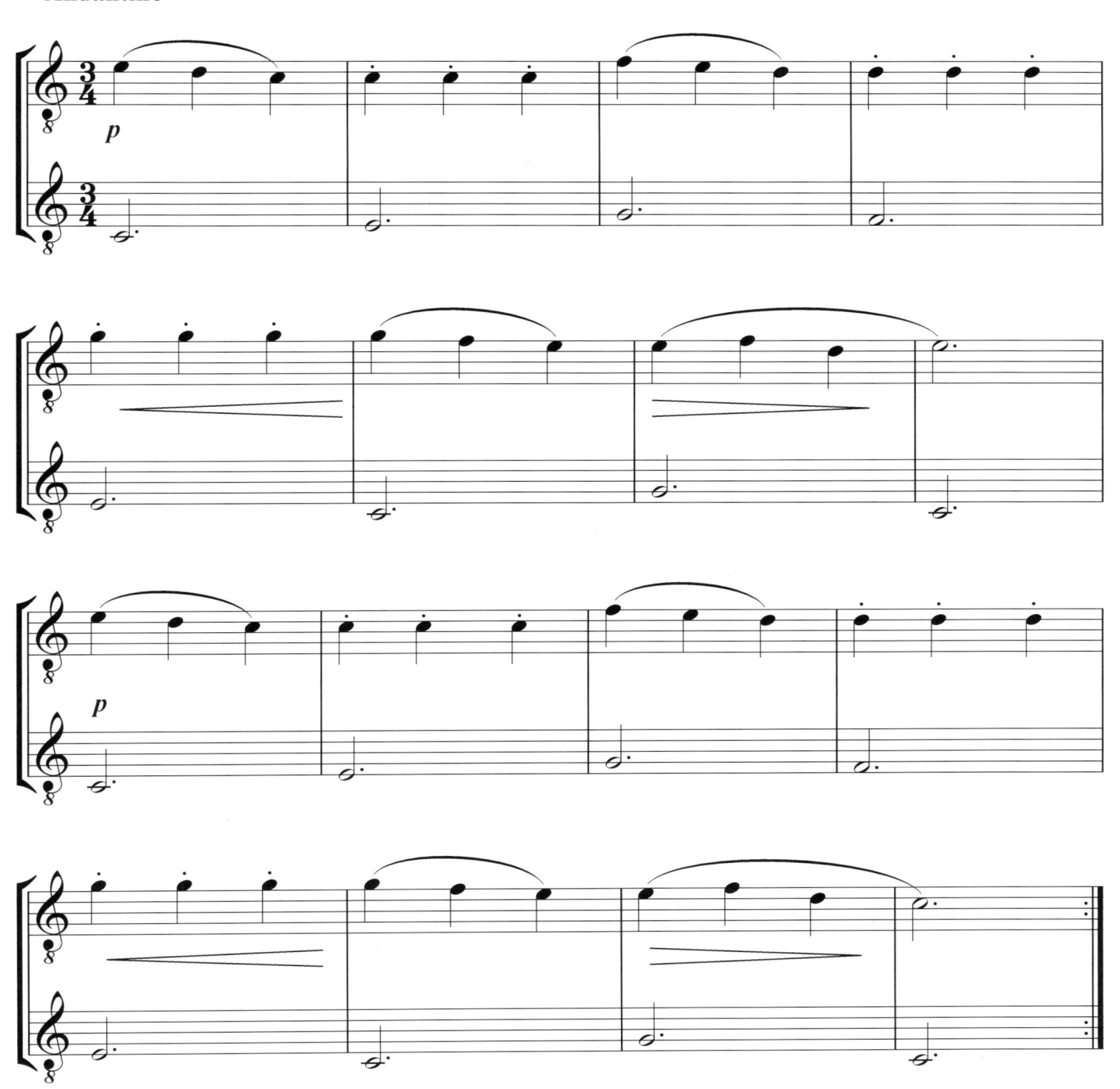

Minuet

C. H. Wilton
(1761-1832)

The student plays the top part.
Notice the phrasing and dynamics as well as the special fingering in bar 9.

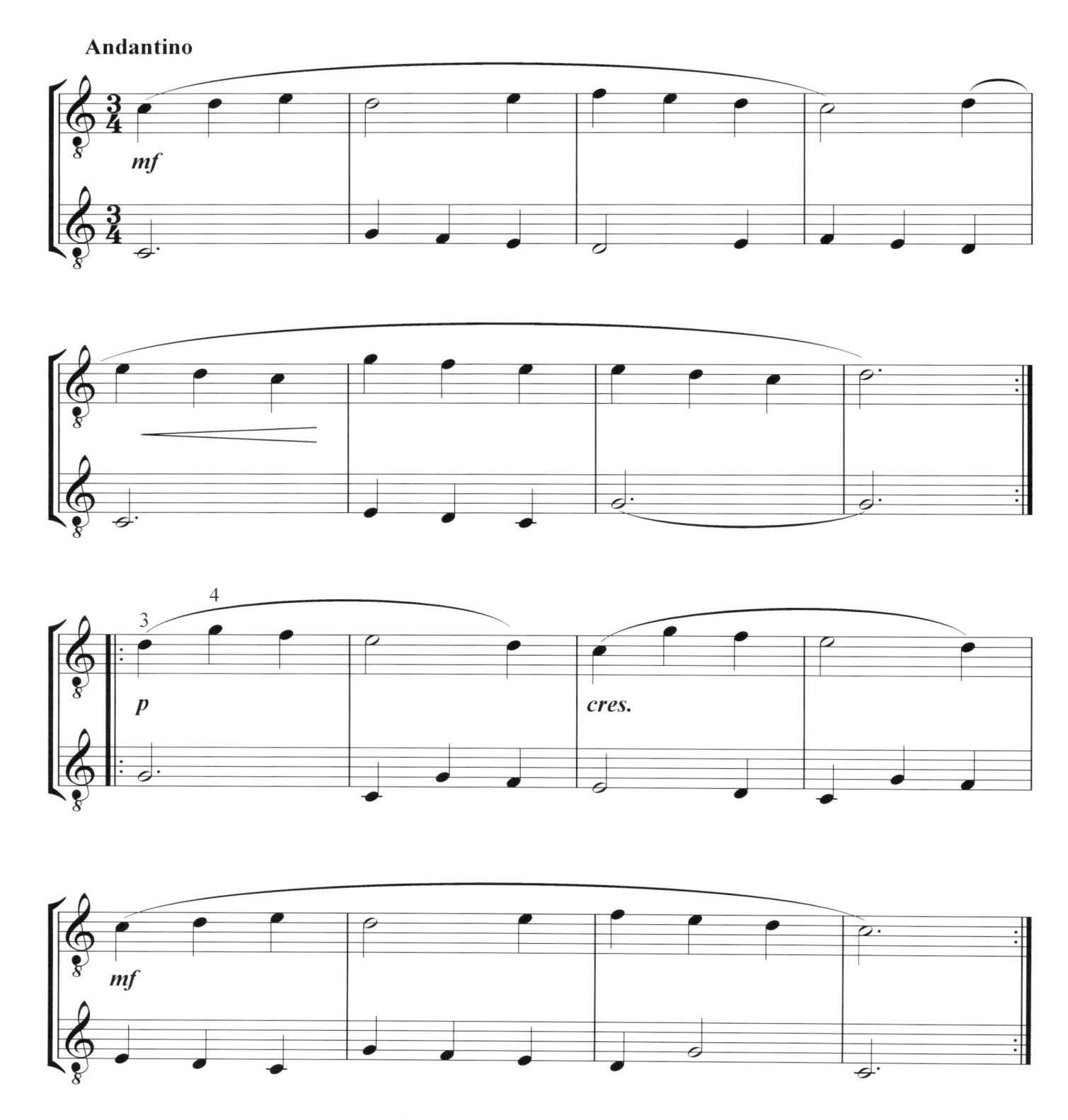

Morning

Anton Diabelli
(1781-1858)

The student plays the top part. Notice the phrasing and dynamics.

New Notes: Open Bass Strings

The lines below the staff are called *ledger lines*.

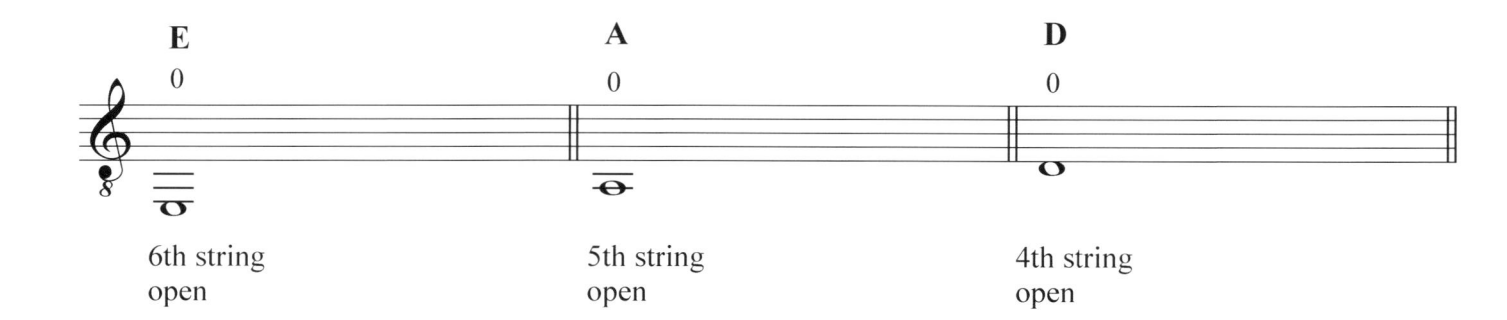

E — 6th string open
A — 5th string open
D — 4th string open

Name the following notes

Name:	**D**	**A**	**E**
Fret:	**0**	**0**	**0**
String:	**4**	**5**	**6**

Name:	**G**	**A**
Fret:	**0**	**2**
String:	**3**	**3**

© Bradford Werner 2017, Victoria, BC, Canada
Free & Premium Sheet Music & Tab: wernerguitareditions.com
Lessons, Pro Video, & Blog: thisisclassicalguitar.com

Etude No. 5 - Waltz

This piece combines melody with bass accompaniment.
The melody (top three strings) should be played as the prominent musical voice.
Sustain the melody notes despite their quarter note value (keep fingers down during each bar).

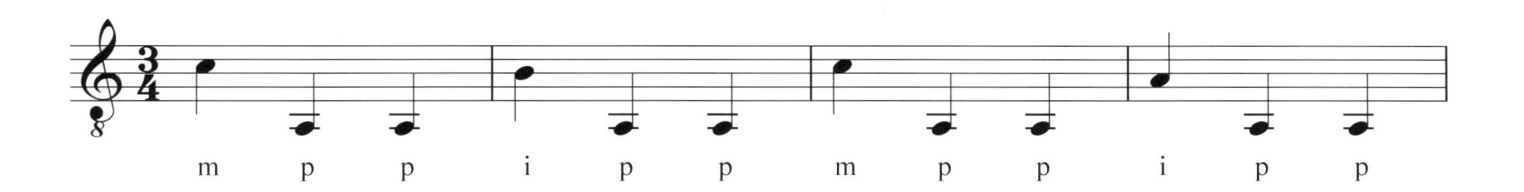

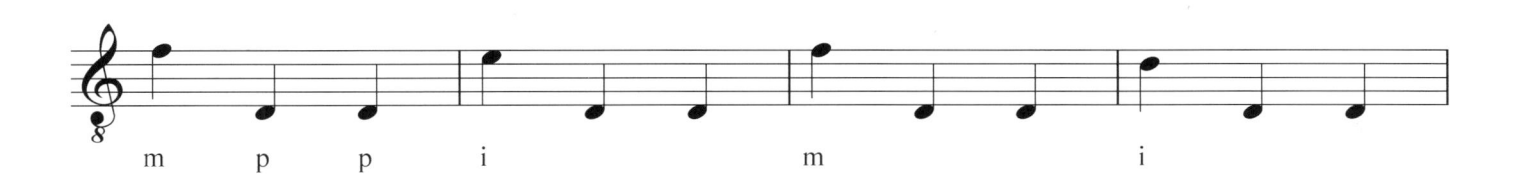

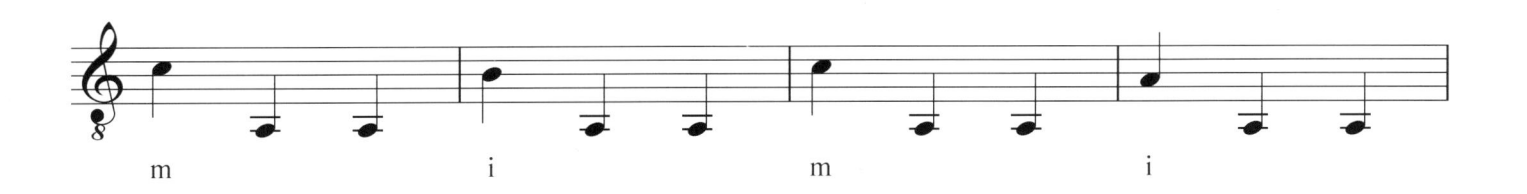

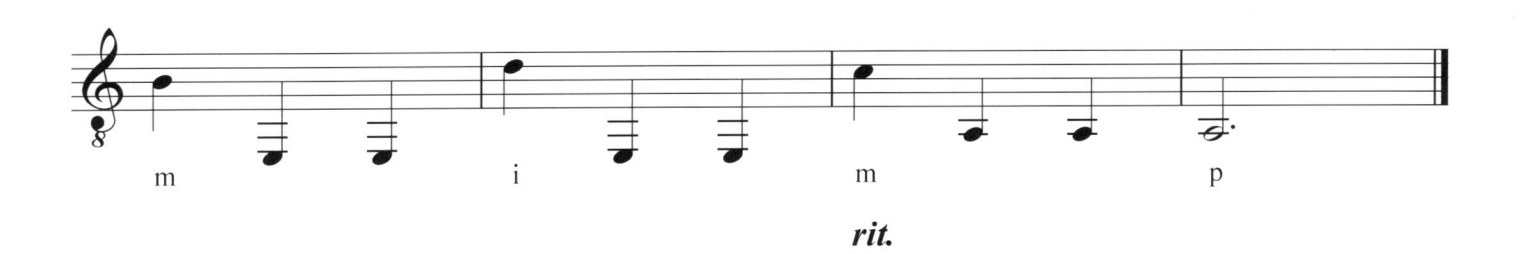

Etude No. 6 - Allegro

As with Etude No. 5, make the melody (higher notes) the prominant voice.
Let the last melody note of each scale run sustain for the entire bar.
I've indicated the sustain in the second bar only.
Allegro indicates a brisk (fast) tempo.

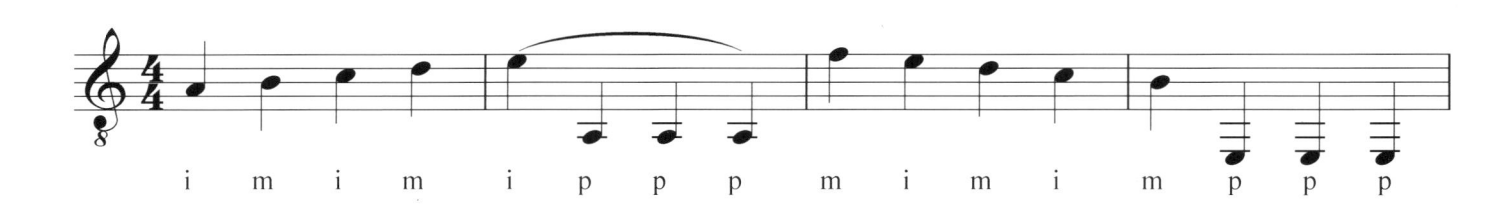

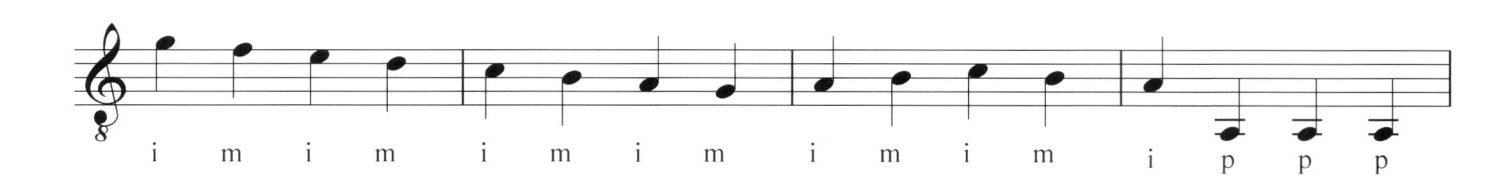

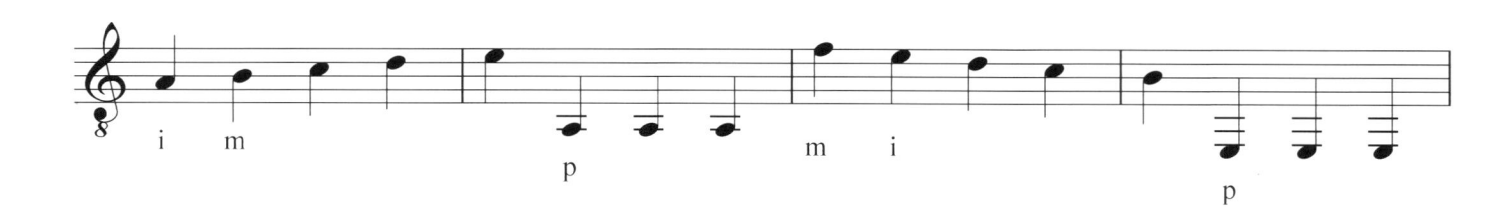

Etude No. 7 - The Lonely Dogwood

This piece introduces the *a* finger during arpeggios. Hold fingers down and let all notes sustain.

New Notes

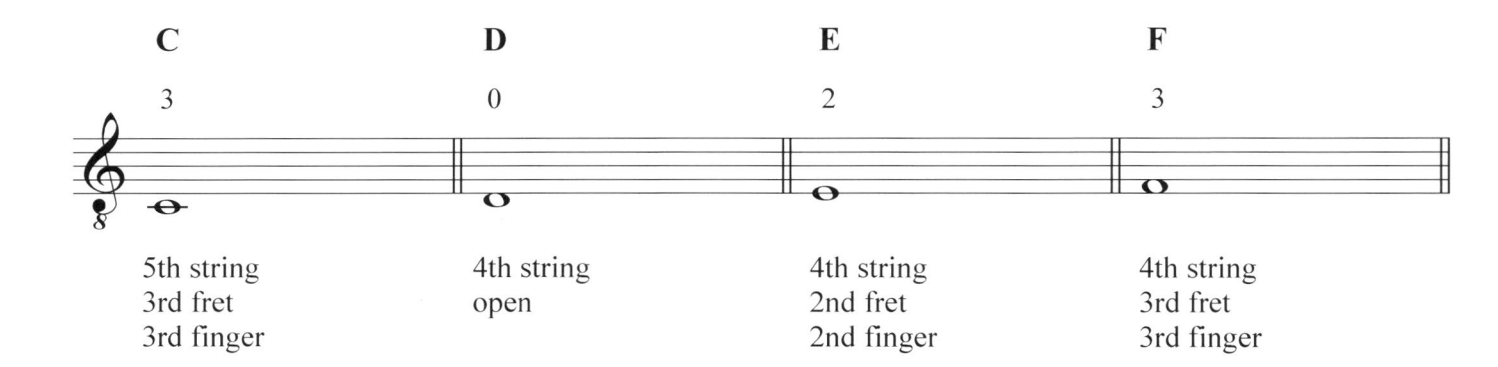

C — 3
5th string
3rd fret
3rd finger

D — 0
4th string
open

E — 2
4th string
2nd fret
2nd finger

F — 3
4th string
3rd fret
3rd finger

Complete the following note names, frets, and strings

Name: **F   E   C**

Fret: **3   2   3**

String: **4   4   5**

Name: **A   F**

Fret: **2   3**

String: **3   4**

© Bradford Werner 2017, Victoria, BC, Canada
Free & Premium Sheet Music & Tab: wernerguitareditions.com
Lessons, Pro Video, & Blog: thisisclassicalguitar.com

Etude No. 8 - Prelude

Hold fingers down and let notes sustain.

C Major Scale

This is a C major scale with repeated half notes.
You will learn more about major scales in Volume Two.

Rest your thumb on the 6th string.
Use i, m the entire time.
Memorize this scale and warm up with it everyday.

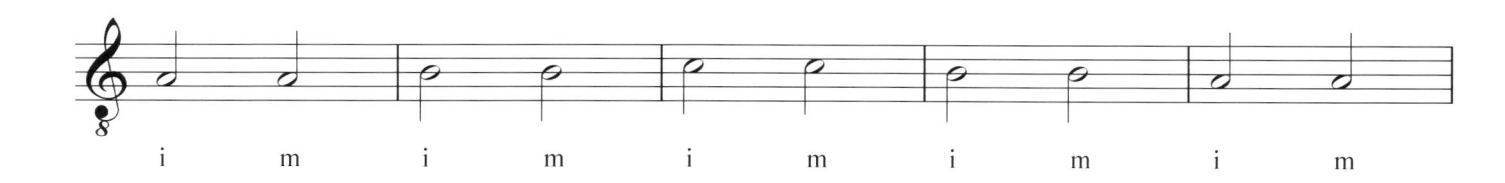

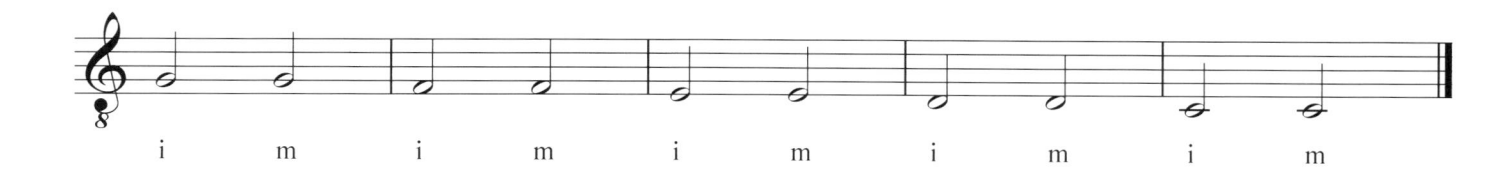

© **Bradford Werner 2017, Victoria, BC, Canada**
Free & Premium Sheet Music & Tab: wernerguitareditions.com
Lessons, Pro Video, & Blog: thisisclassicalguitar.com

Note Review

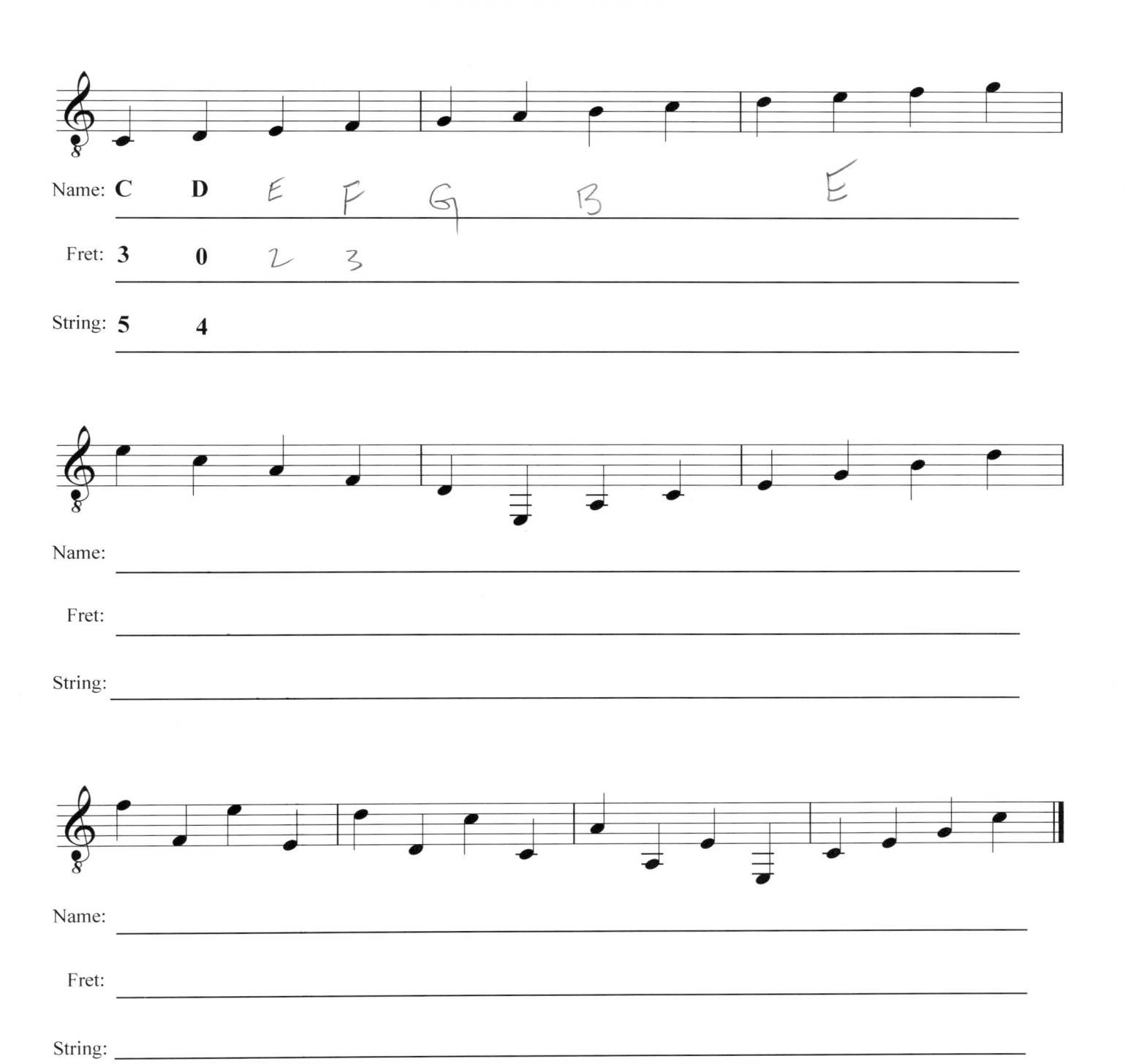

Name: **C** **D** E F G B E

Fret: **3** **0** 2 3

String: **5** **4**

Name:

Fret:

String:

Name:

Fret:

String:

Eighth Notes

Both exercises below contain the same rhythmic pattern but indicate different counting.
Become comfortable with both systems of counting. Count out loud as you play (+ = and).
Notice that eighth notes are connected with *beams*.

Exercise No. 1
Count the written numbers and say "and" for the plus sign.

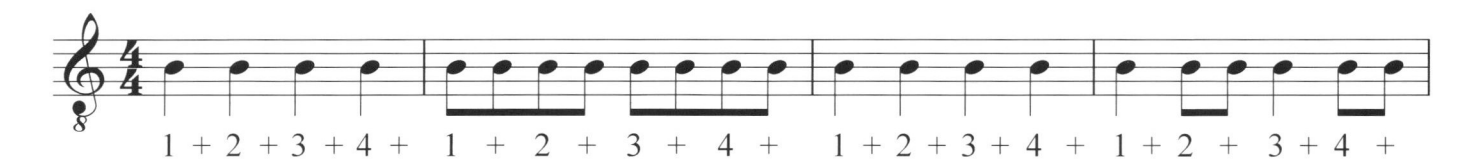

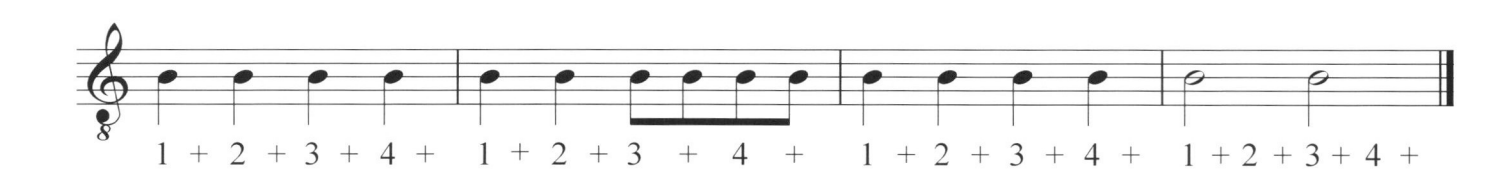

Exercise No. 2
Only count the written numbers (do not say "and" between the quarter beats).

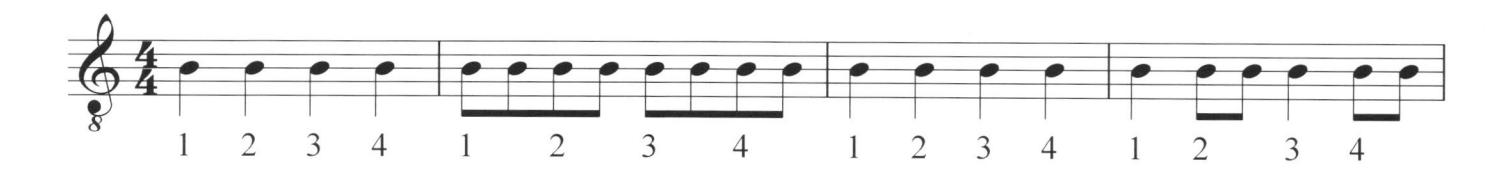

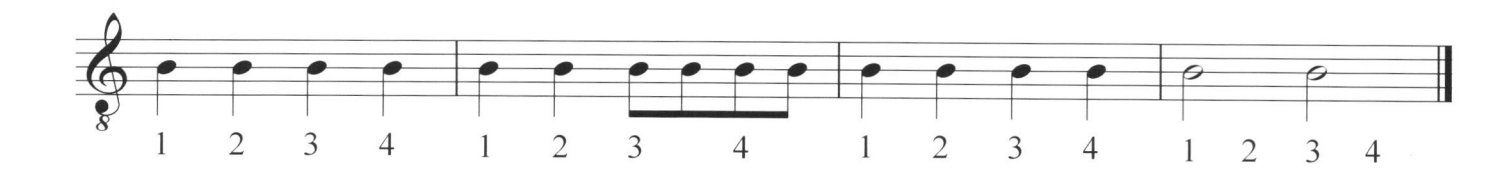

© Bradford Werner 2017, Victoria, BC, Canada
Free & Premium Sheet Music & Tab: wernerguitareditions.com
Lessons, Pro Video, & Blog: thisisclassicalguitar.com

Minuet

The student plays the top part.

James Hook
(1746-1827)

Etude No. 9 - Glass

Let all notes sustain.

Vsi so venci vejli
(All the Wreaths are White)

Traditional Slovenian
Transcribed by Uroš Barič

Notice the changing time signature and eighth notes.
Thanks to my friend, guitarist Uroš Barič for sending me this beautiful song.
Uroš runs some fantastic wesbites and has a record label: urosbaric.com
Play this song slowly and legato aiming for the first beat of each bar.
I suggest the teacher join in with chord accompaniment on the repeat.

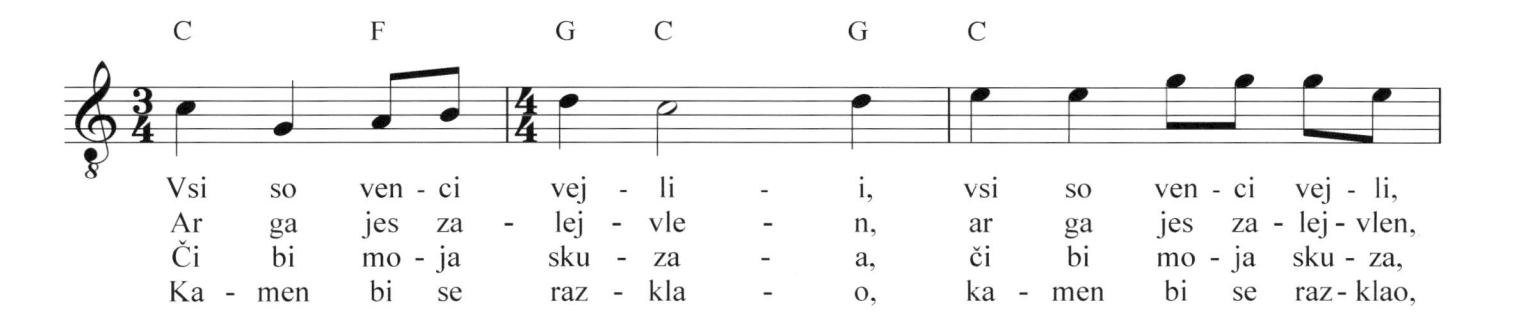

Vsi so ven-ci vej-li - i, vsi so ven-ci vej-li,
Ar ga jes za-lej-vle - n, ar ga jes za-lej-vlen,
Či bi mo-ja sku-za - a, či bi mo-ja sku-za,
Ka-men bi se raz-kla - o, ka-men bi se raz-klao,

vsi so-o ven-ci vej-li, sa-mo moj ze-le-ni.
ar ga-a jes za-lej-vlen, ssvo-ji-mi sku-za-mi.
či bi-i mo-ja sku-za, na ka-men spa-dno-la.
ka-me-n bi se raz-klao na dvou-je, na trou-je.

© Bradford Werner 2017, Victoria, BC, Canada
Free & Premium Sheet Music & Tab: wernerguitareditions.com
Lessons, Pro Video, & Blog: thisisclassicalguitar.com

Flow Gently, Sweet Afton

Scottish Folk Song

The student plays the top part. The melody is in both parts so phrase together.

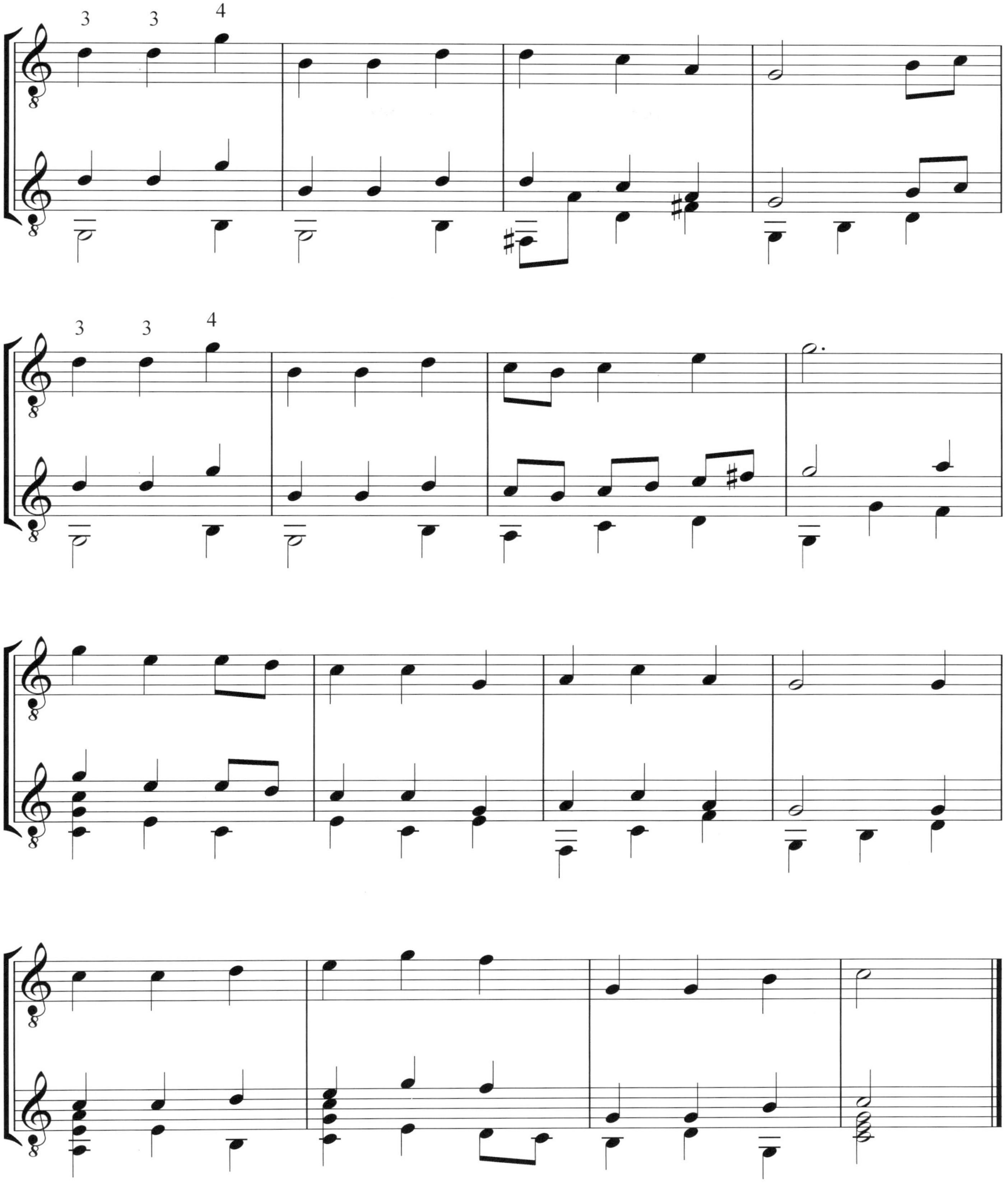

Two Voice Textures

Multiple musical lines can be written and played simultaneously.
When two voices are written, each voice accounts for all the beats in the bar.
This allows composers to write out exactly how long each note should sustain.
Let's first look at the voices separately and then combine them into one staff.

Voice One (upper)

Voice Two (lower)

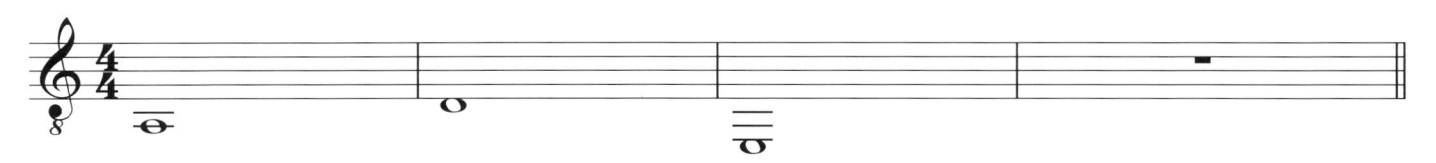

Both voices on the same staff (two-part texture)
Notice the rests in each voice account for all beats in the bar.

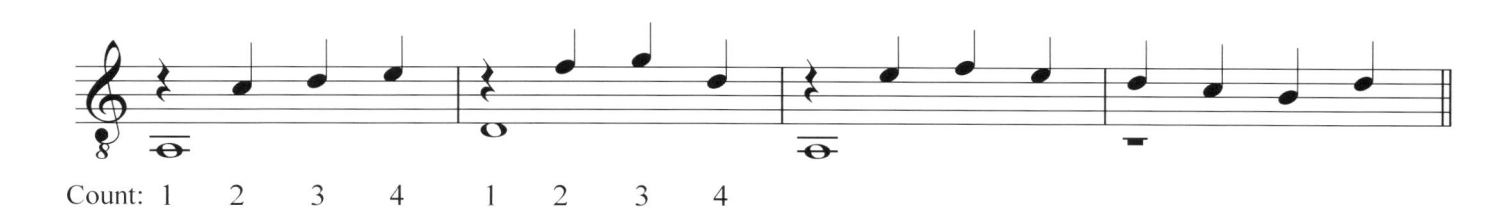

Count: 1   2   3   4   1   2   3   4

Etude No. 10 - The Swan

Different stem directions help keep the voices separate.
Notice the special fingering needed to play legato from G to D.

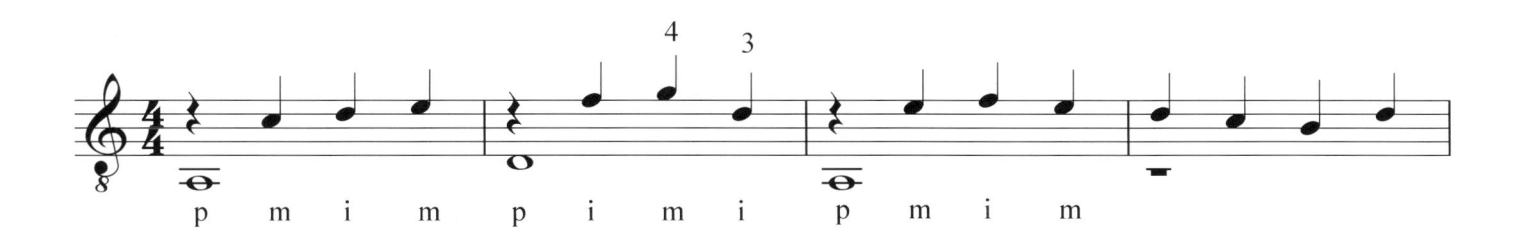

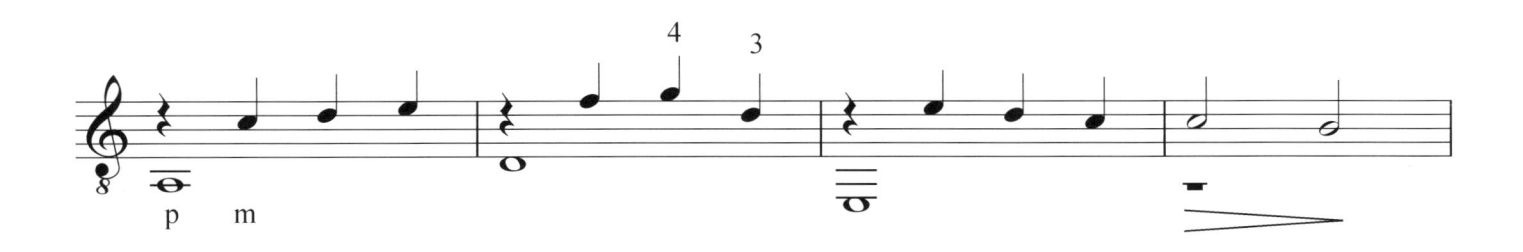

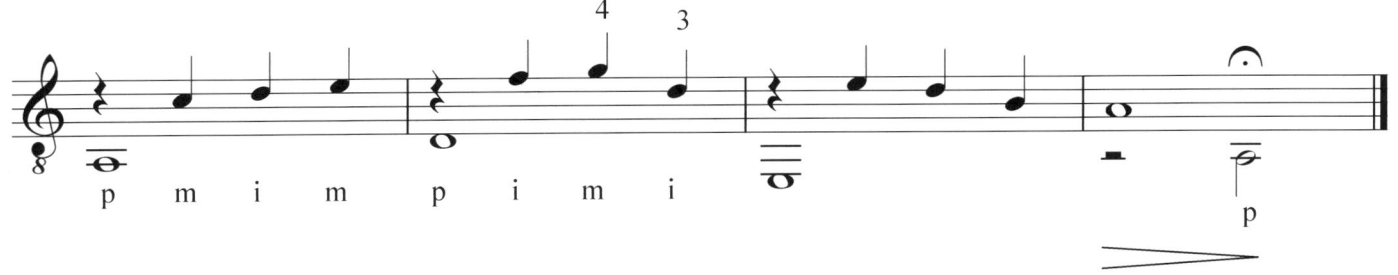

Etude No. 11 - The Old Douglas Fir

Play the melody (stems up) on its own a few times before including the bass notes.
Notice how two notes from separate voices are played at the same time in bar 8 and bar 16.

i p m i p m

Dotted Quarter Notes

A dot after a note adds half of its value to its length.
A dotted quarter note equals one and a half beats.

$$\text{♩.} = \text{♩} + \text{♪}$$

Example: Deck the Halls

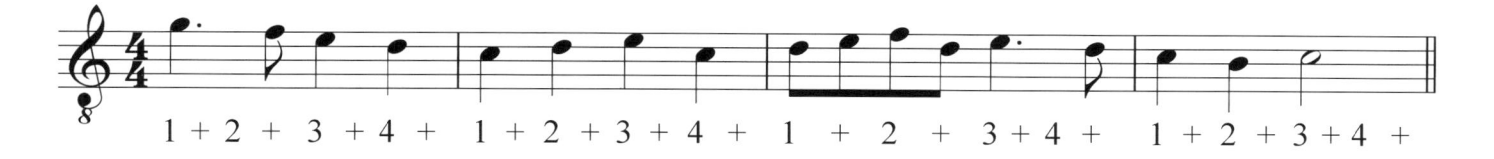

1 + 2 + 3 + 4 +   1 + 2 + 3 + 4 +   1 + 2 + 3 + 4 +   1 + 2 + 3 + 4 +

Count out loud as written (say the "and")

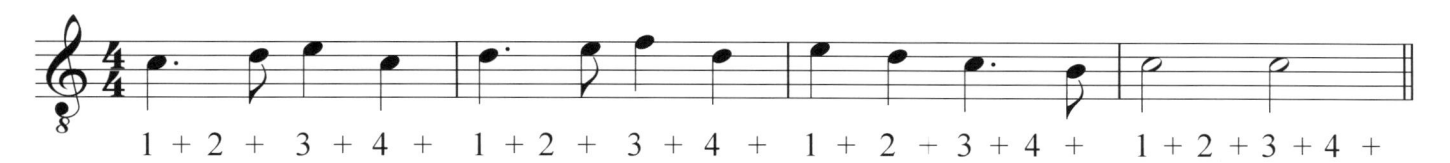

1 + 2 + 3 + 4 +   1 + 2 + 3 + 4 +   1 + 2 + 3 + 4 +   1 + 2 + 3 + 4 +

Count out loud as written (do <u>not</u> say "and" this time)

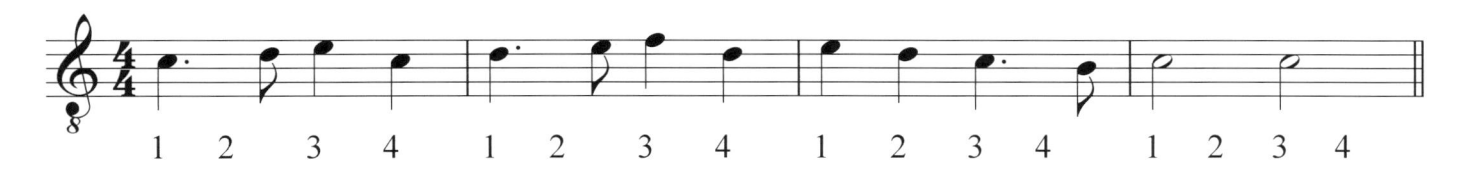

1 2 3 4   1 2 3 4   1 2 3 4   1 2 3 4

© Bradford Werner 2017, Victoria, BC, Canada
Free & Premium Sheet Music & Tab: wernerguitareditions.com
Lessons, Pro Video, & Blog: thisisclassicalguitar.com

Во поле берёзка стояла

(Little Birch Tree in the Field)

Russian Folk Song

Notice the time signature for this piece has only two beats per bar.
Thanks to my friend, guitarist Natasha Pashchenko, for suggesting this one!

The Skye Boat Song

Scottish Folk Song

The student plays the melody. The teacher accompanies with chords.
D.C. al Fine - Return to beginning and play to the *Fine*.

Fifth String Notes

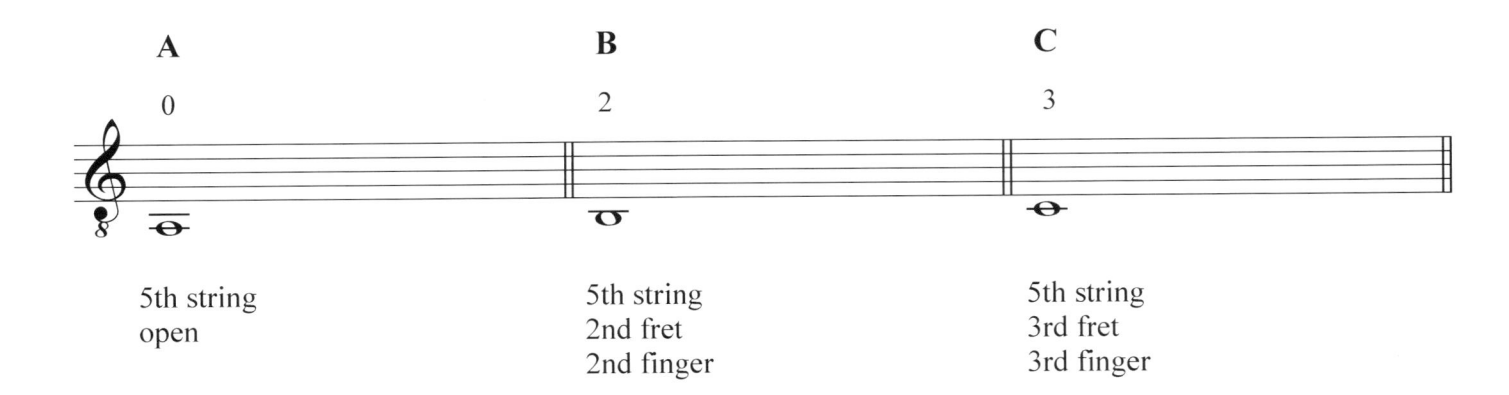

A   **B**   **C**
0   2   3

5th string open

5th string
2nd fret
2nd finger

5th string
3rd fret
3rd finger

Name the following notes

Name:	**A**	**B**	**C**
Fret:	**0**	**2**	**3**
String:	**5**	**5**	**5**

Name:	**A**	**F**
Fret:	**2**	**3**
String:	**3**	**4**

© **Bradford Werner 2017, Victoria, BC, Canada**
Free & Premium Sheet Music & Tab: wernerguitareditions.com
Lessons, Pro Video, & Blog: thisisclassicalguitar.com

Note Review

Name: **A**　**B**

Fret: **0**　**2**

String: **5**　**5**

Name:

Fret:

String:

Name:

Fret:

String:

© Bradford Werner 2017, Victoria, BC, Canada
Free & Premium Sheet Music & Tab: wernerguitareditions.com
Lessons, Pro Video, & Blog: thisisclassicalguitar.com

Capriccio

Johann Anton Logy
(1650-1721)

The student plays the **bottom** part using *p* throughout.

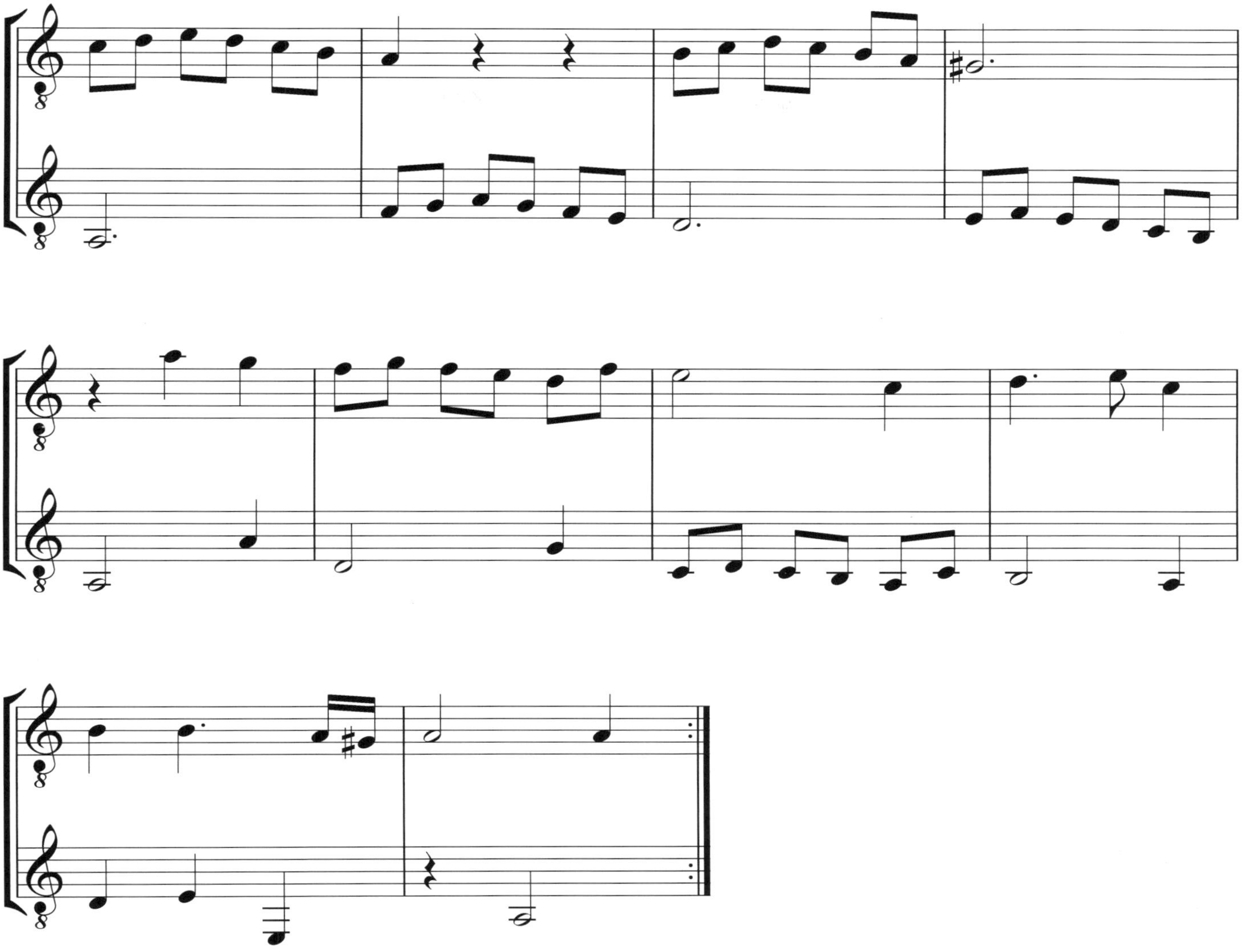

Sixth String Notes

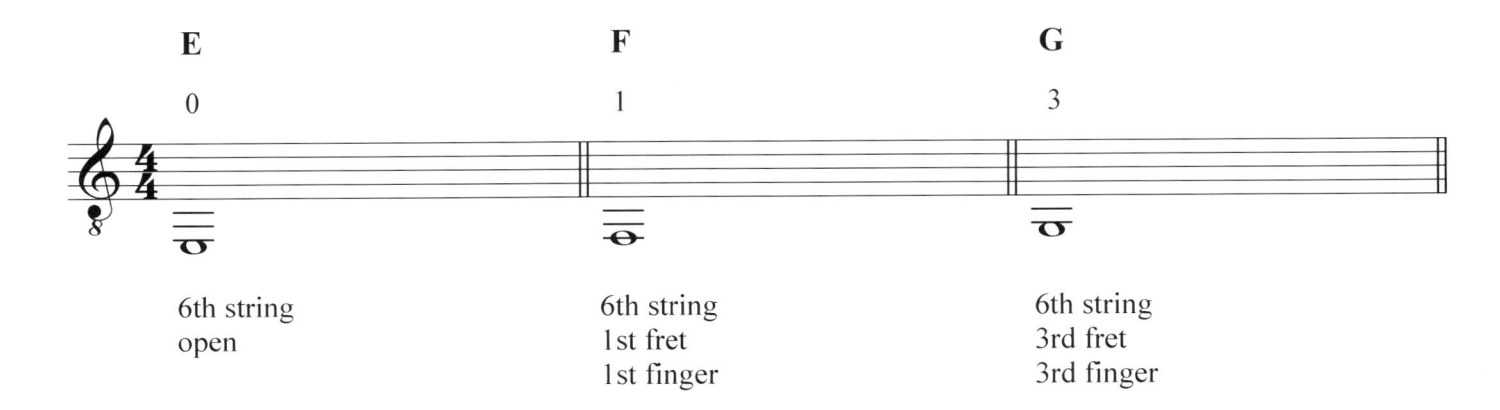

E   **F**   **G**
0   1   3

6th string open   6th string 1st fret 1st finger   6th string 3rd fret 3rd finger

Name the following notes

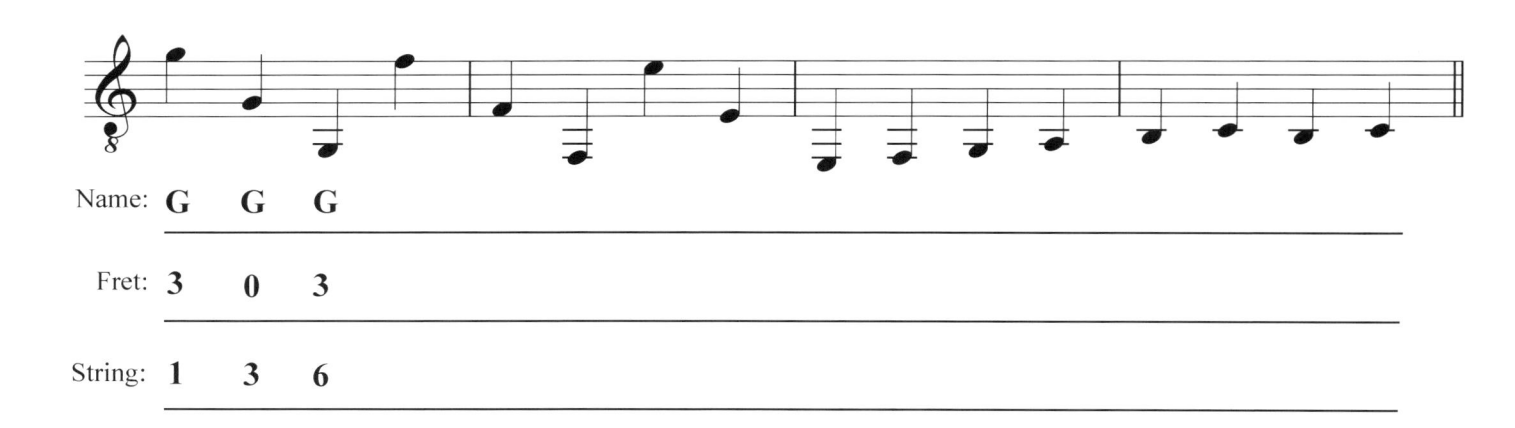

Name: **E**   **F**   **G**

Fret: **0**   **1**   **3**

String: **6**   **6**   **6**

Name: **G**   **G**   **G**

Fret: **3**   **0**   **3**

String: **1**   **3**   **6**

© **Bradford Werner 2017, Victoria, BC, Canada**
Free & Premium Sheet Music & Tab: wernerguitareditions.com
Lessons, Pro Video, & Blog: thisisclassicalguitar.com

Note Review

Say the note names out loud as you play.
Use i, m fingering on the top five strings and thumb for the 6th string.
When playing with i, m, rest your thumb on the 6th string.

Note Naming

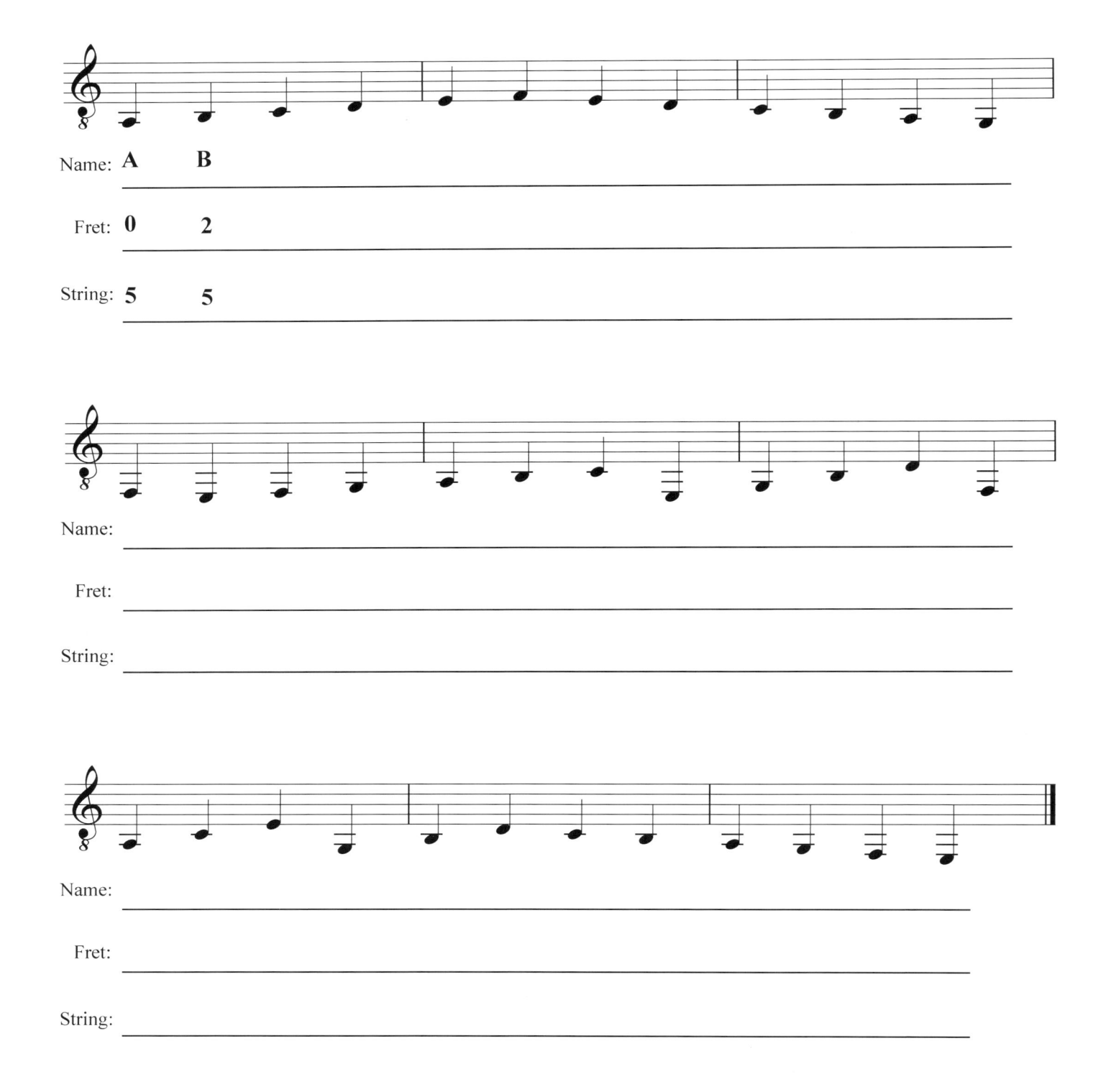

Name: **A** **B**

Fret: **0** **2**

String: **5** **5**

Name:

Fret:

String:

Name:

Fret:

String:

Leyenda Theme

Isaac Albeniz
(1860-1909)

This piece is notated in one voice for simplicity. Let all notes sustain.
Notice the special fingering to play from E to B legato on the 4th and 5th string.
The time signature has 6 quarter notes beats for each bar with the strongest beats on 1 and 4.

p m p m p m

© Bradford Werner 2017, Victoria, BC, Canada
Free & Premium Sheet Music & Tab: wernerguitareditions.com
Lessons, Pro Video, & Blog: thisisclassicalguitar.com

Accidentals

♯ **Sharps** raise the pitch by a half-step (up one fret).

♭ **Flats** lower the pitch by a half-step (down one fret).

♮ **Naturals** return the note to its regular pitch.

G Chromatic Scale
In the below scale each new string is marked with a string number with a circle around it.
The fingering matches the fret number for this scale so use your third finger on D and G.
When flats are used on open string notes the flat note must be found on an adjacent string.

The Musical Alphabet
There are 12 notes in the traditional musical alphabet. Some notes have two different names
but share the same pitch (sound), these are called *enharmonic notes* (indicted with slash marks).

Musical Alphabet:	A	A#/Bb	B	C	C#/Db	D	D#/Eb	E	F	F#/Gb	G	G#/Ab	A
With Sharps:	A	A#	B	C	C#	D	D#	E	F	F#	G	G#	A
With Flats:	A	Bb	B	C	Db	D	Eb	E	F	Gb	G	Ab	A

© **Bradford Werner 2017**, Victoria, BC, Canada
Free & Premium Sheet Music & Tab: wernerguitareditions.com
Lessons, Pro Video, & Blog: thisisclassicalguitar.com

E Chromatic Scale

This E chromatic scale goes up to the highest note in first postion.
Say the note names out loud as you play.

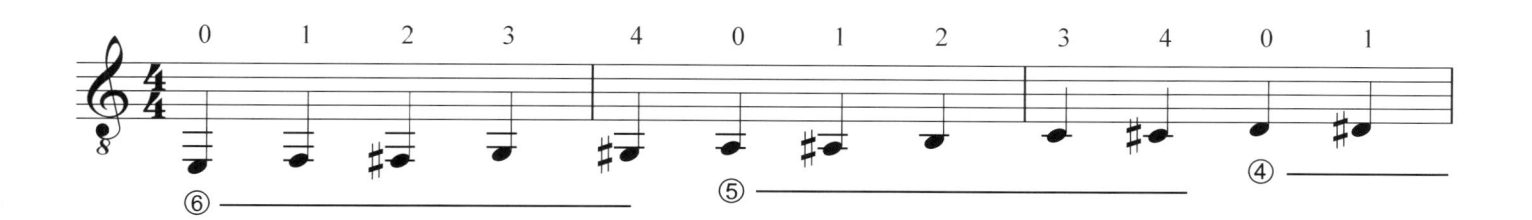

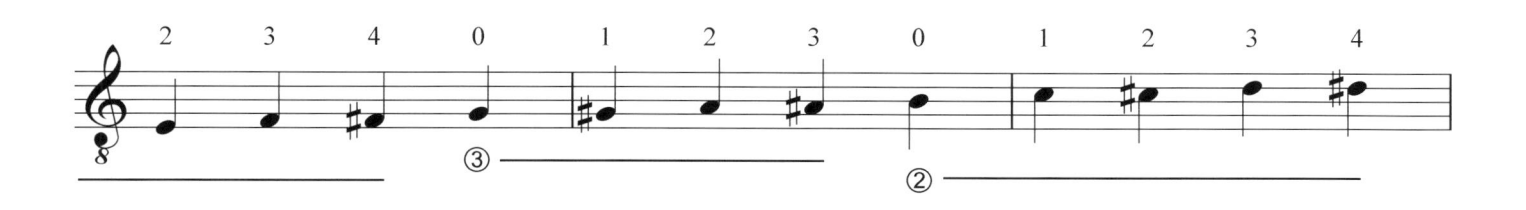

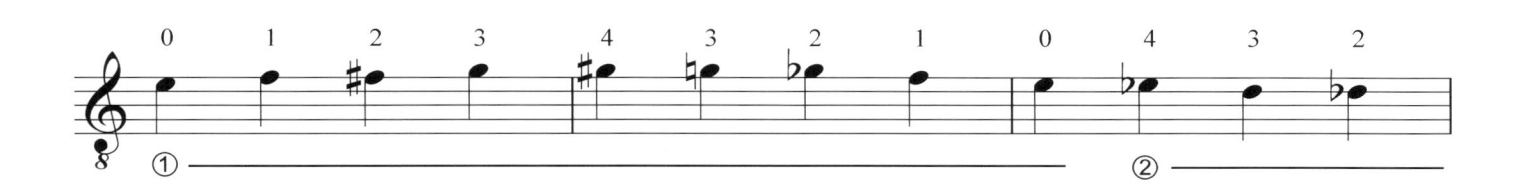

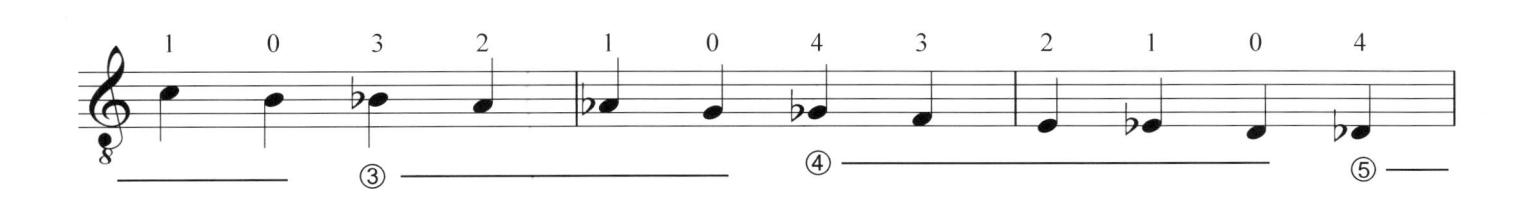

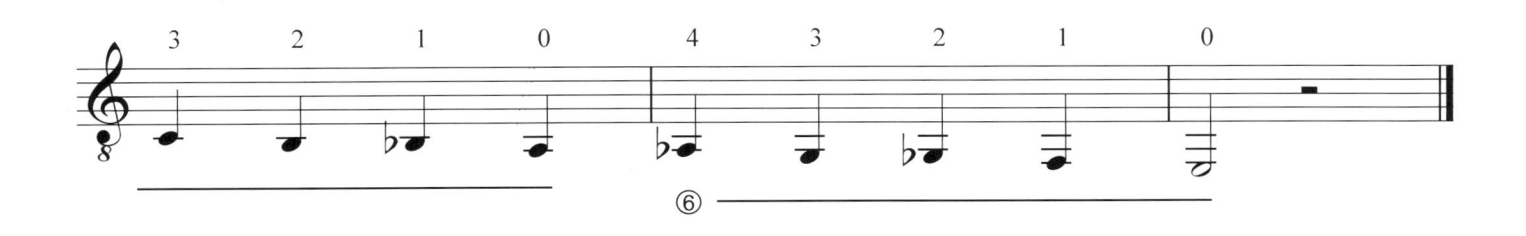

Greensleeves

Traditional

The student plays the melody. The teacher accompanies with chords.
Accidentals (sharps and flats) last for the entire bar. For example, the G#
in the first bar of the third line also applies to the G on the last beat of that bar.

Minuet in G

The student plays the upper part.
Play quarter notes slightly detached and eighth notes legato.
(Key signatures will be covered in Volume Two)

Christian Petzold (1677-1733)
From J.S. Bach's Notenbuch der Anna Magdalena Bach

Tutú Maramba

Brazilian Folksong

Following the fingering very carefully for a legato sound.

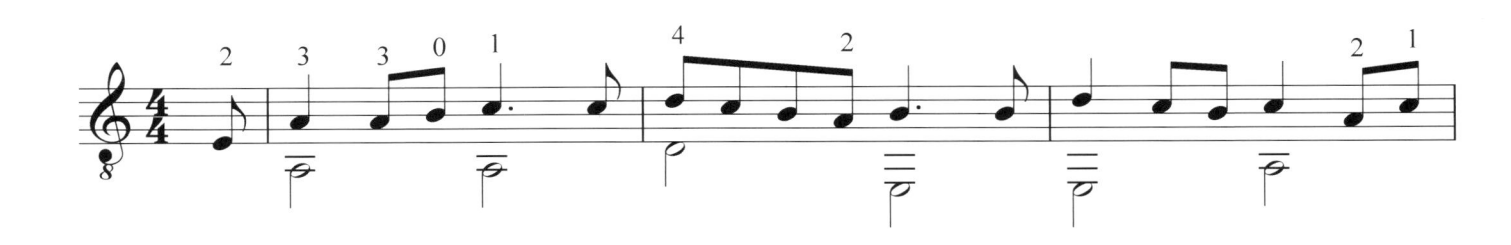

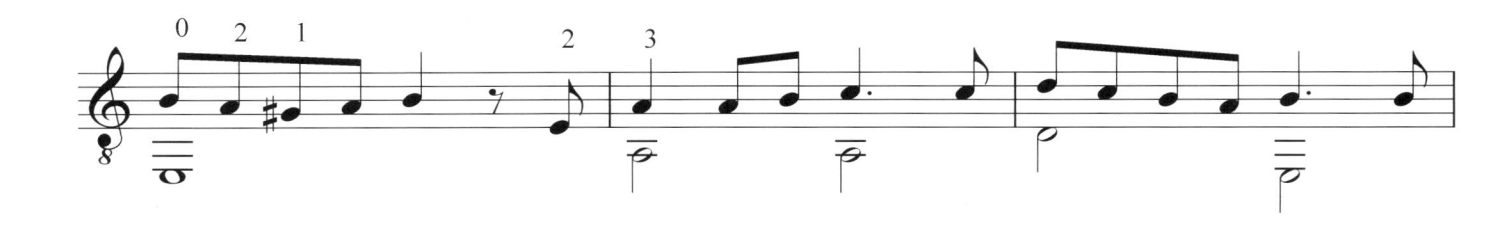

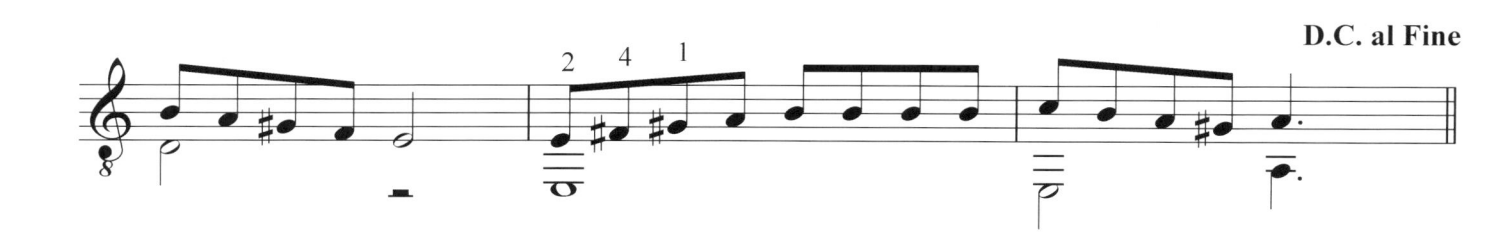

Django Swing

This fun piece is influenced by famous jazz guitarist Django Reinhardt.

Etude No. 12 - à la Brouwer

This piece is influenced by the famous guitar composer Leo Brouwer (b.1939).
Use *p* for all bass notes (stems going down) and *i, m* for the repeated accompaniment.
You may want to begin by counting the eighth notes as: 1-2-3 1-2-3 1-2 as the beaming suggests.

© Bradford Werner 2017, Victoria, BC, Canada

Free & Premium Sheet Music & Tab: wernerguitareditions.com
Lessons, Pro Video, & Blog: thisisclassicalguitar.com

Minuet

The student should play the upper part.

Johann Krieger
(1651-1735)

Fine

D.C. al Fine

Sor Study No. 1, Op. 60

Fernando Sor
(1778-1839)

Although written in one voice, this study is more complex than it looks.
There are many possible right hand fingerings for this piece,
I've focused on using p, i, m for the purposes of this book.

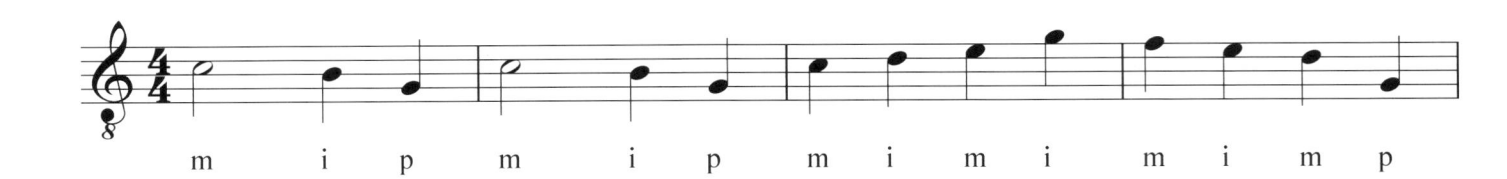

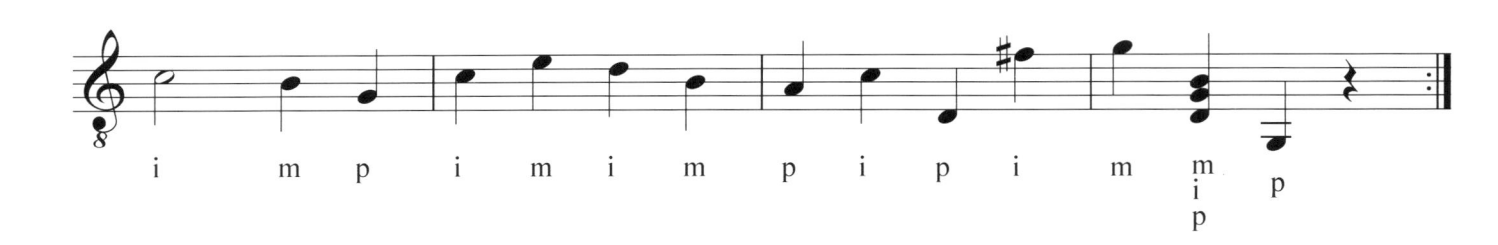

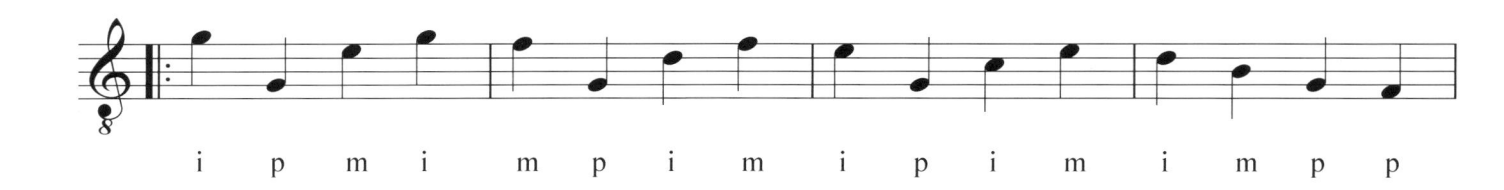

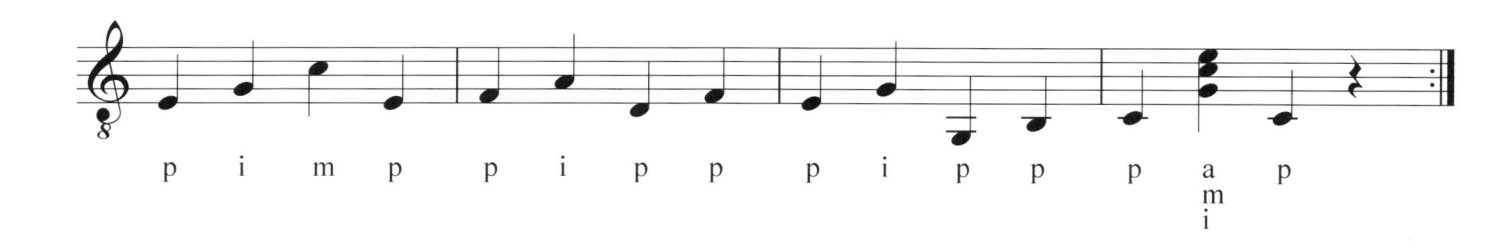

Siciliano

Matteo Carcassi
(1792-1853)

Ties join together the rhythm of two notes of the same pitch.
Sustain for the full value of both notes (but do not re-pluck the 2nd note).

Übungen auf der E saite

Johann Kaspar Mertz
(1806-1856)

Exercise on the E String from Mertz's Method: *Schule für die Guitare*
Sometimes notes are shared by more than one voice to indicate
rhythmic value and voice independence while presenting clear beat structure.

Etude No. 13 - Farewell

Triplets: Three notes evenly spaced within one beat (indicated by the bracket).
The first note of each triplet is the melody. Let all notes sustain.

Chord Accompaniment Section

Before learning fingerstyle accompaniment some basic strumming patterns will be played.

Chord Diagrams
- Vertical lines = the strings
- Horizontal lines = the frets

- The string on the left is the 6th string (bass)
- Do not strum strings that have an X.
- The numbers below are the fingering.

- E minor = Strum the top three open strings
- Strum down from the 3rd string to the 1st using your thumb or a pick.

E Minor (Em)

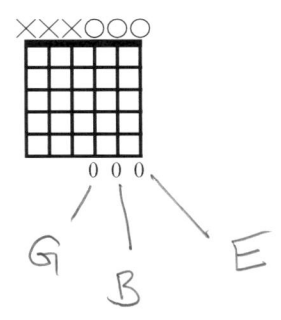

Hey, Ho, Nobody Home
- Strum four beats for each bar as indicated by the slash marks (do not read the notes).
- Count out loud as you play.
- The teacher plays or sings the melody.

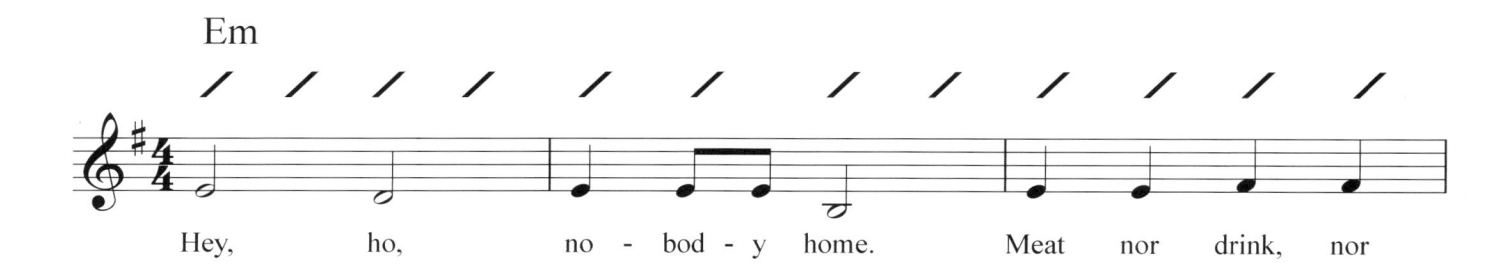

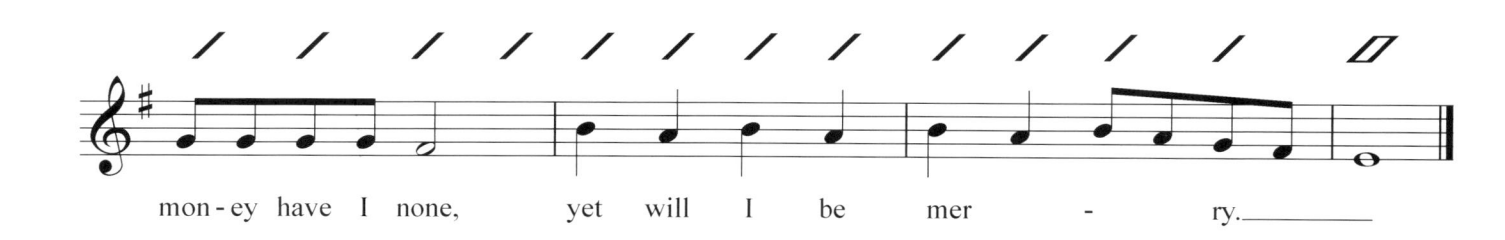

Hey, ho, no-bod-y home. Meat nor drink, nor mon-ey have I none, yet will I be mer - ry.

© Bradford Werner 2017, Victoria, BC, Canada
Free & Premium Sheet Music & Tab: wernerguitareditions.com
Lessons, Pro Video, & Blog: thisisclassicalguitar.com

Frère Jacques / Brother John

Traditional
France

The student strums a G Major chord (do not play the notes).
Strum four beats for each bar and sing the lyrics.

G Major Chord: 1st string, 3rd fret, 3rd finger. Strum the top three strings.

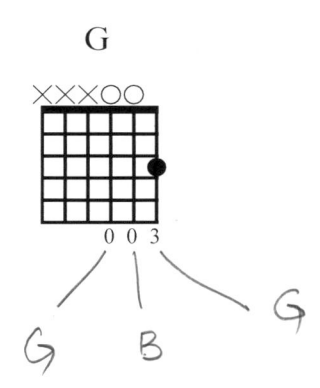

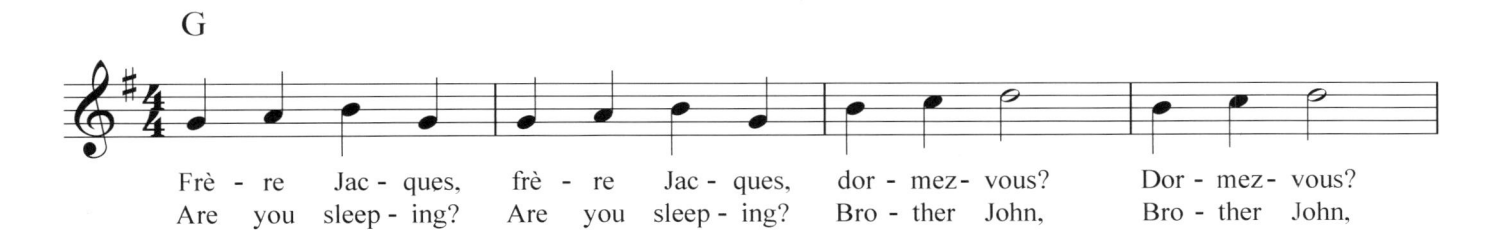

G

G — B — G

G

Frè - re Jac - ques, frè - re Jac - ques, dor - mez - vous? Dor - mez - vous?
Are you sleep - ing? Are you sleep - ing? Bro - ther John, Bro - ther John,

Son - nez les ma - ti - nes! son nez les ma - ti - nes! Ding, dang, dong. Ding, dang, dong.
Morning bells are ring - ing! Morning bells are ring - ing!

© Bradford Werner 2017, Victoria, BC, Canada
Free & Premium Sheet Music & Tab: wernerguitareditions.com
Lessons, Pro Video, & Blog: thisisclassicalguitar.com

London Bridge

Traditional
England

The student strums the chords with four beats per bar and sings.
If no chord is shown, continue strumming the previous chord.

C Major: 2nd string, 1st fret, 1st finger. Strum the top three strings.

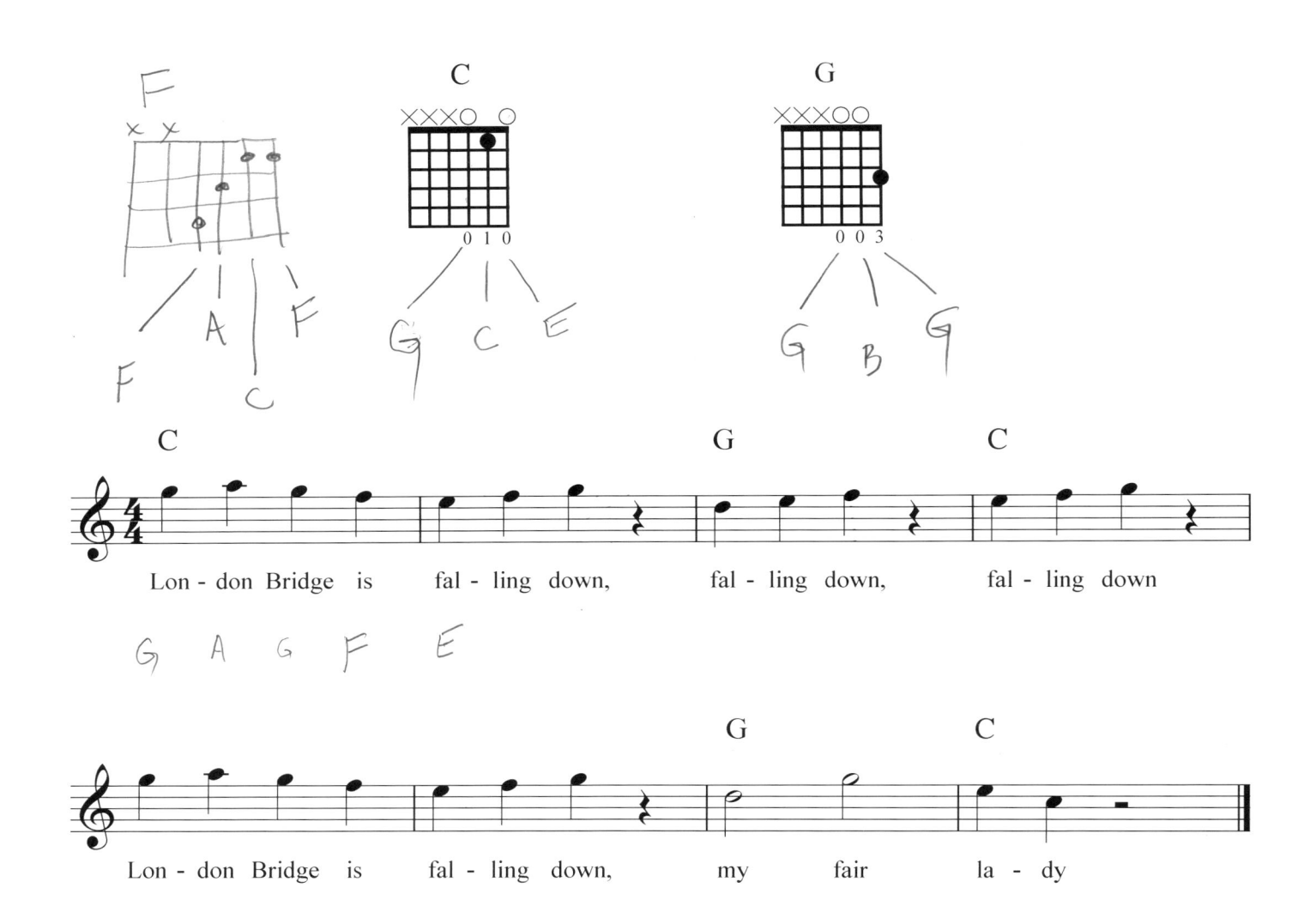

C	G

C | | G | C
Lon - don Bridge is fal - ling down, fal - ling down, fal - ling down

C | | G | C
Lon - don Bridge is fal - ling down, my fair la - dy

© **Bradford Werner 2017**, Victoria, BC, Canada
Free & Premium Sheet Music & Tab: wernerguitareditions.com
Lessons, Pro Video, & Blog: thisisclassicalguitar.com

Amazing Grace

Traditional Hymn
Words: John Newton

Strum the chords with three beats per bar.
D Chord - Follow the chord diagram and strum four strings.

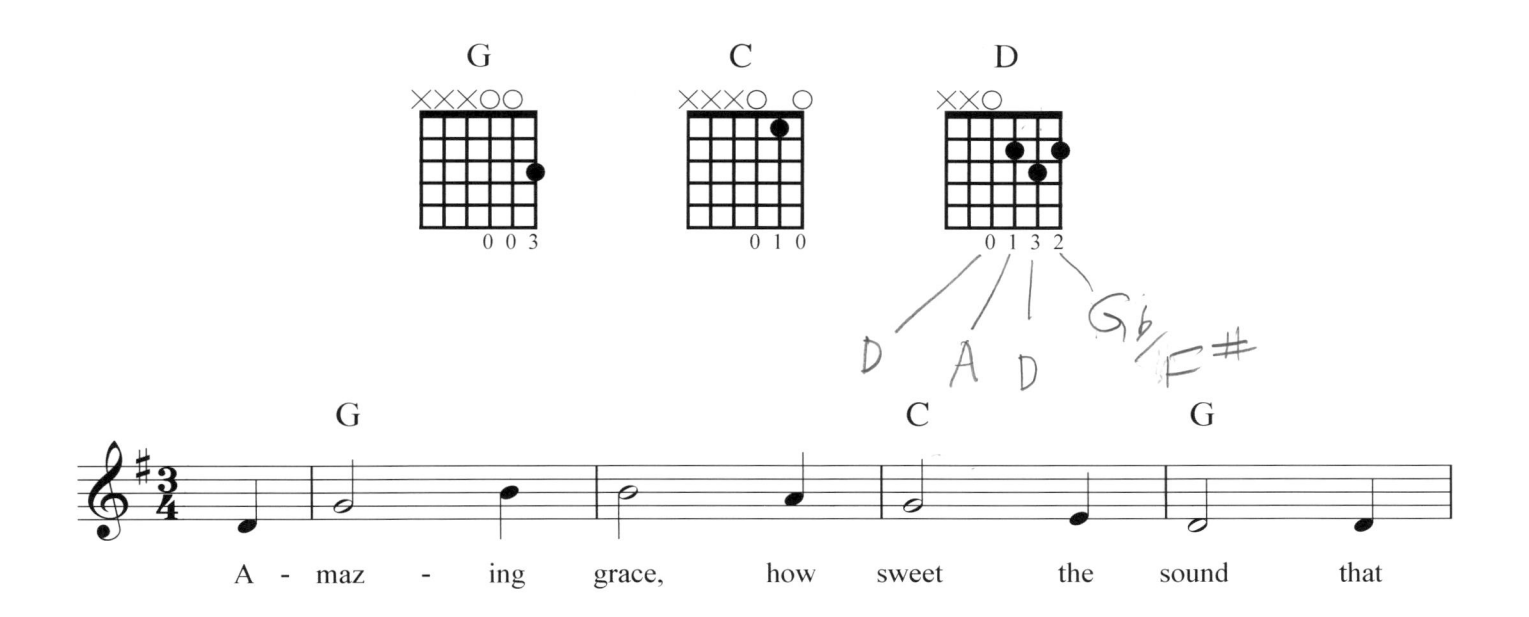

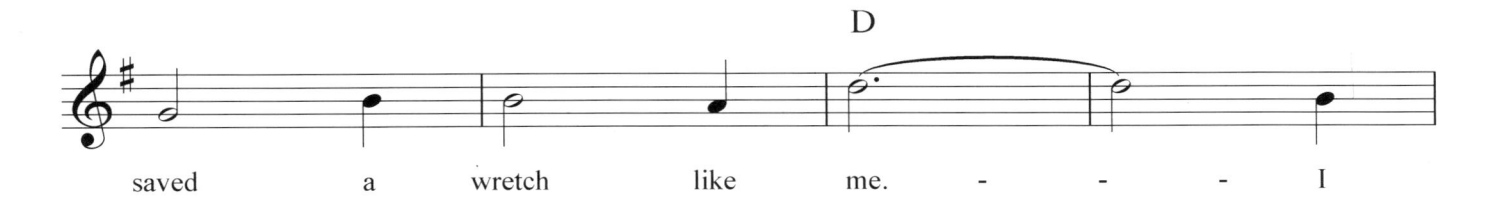

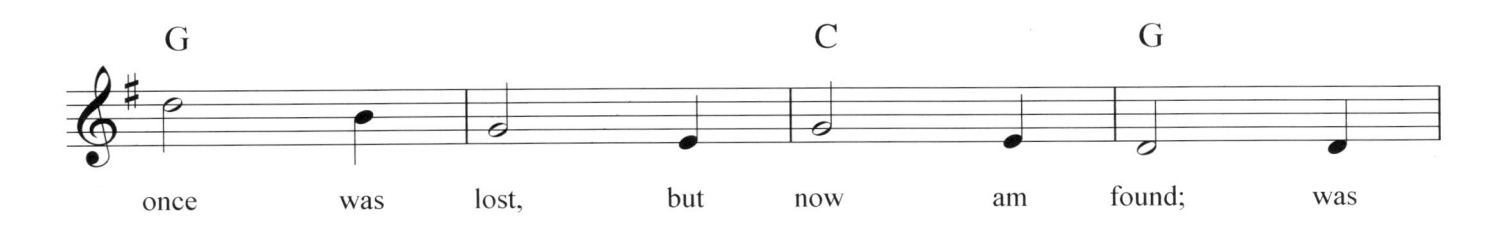

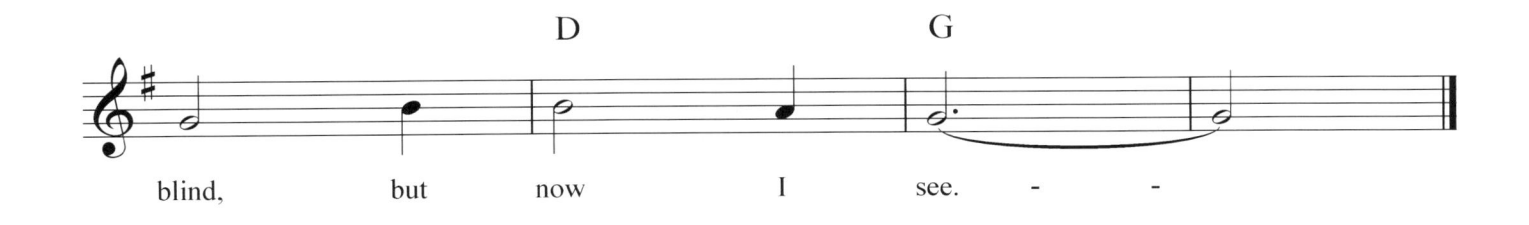

G — xxxOO, 003
C — xxxO O, 010
D — xxO, 0132 (D A D Gb/F#)

| G | | C | G |
A - maz - ing grace, how sweet the sound that

| | D | |
saved a wretch like me. — — — I

| G | C | G |
once was lost, but now am found; was

| D | G | |
blind, but now I see. — —

© **Bradford Werner 2017**, Victoria, BC, Canada
Free & Premium Sheet Music & Tab: wernerguitareditions.com
Lessons, Pro Video, & Blog: thisisclassicalguitar.com

Red River Valley

Traditional
North American

Strum the chords using the below pattern (count four beats per bar).
Slighty swing/relax the eighth note.

Downstrum = ⊓ Upstrum = ∨

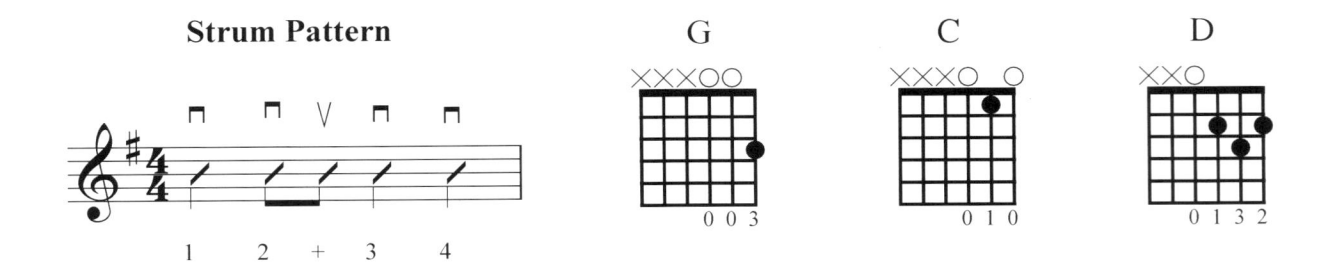

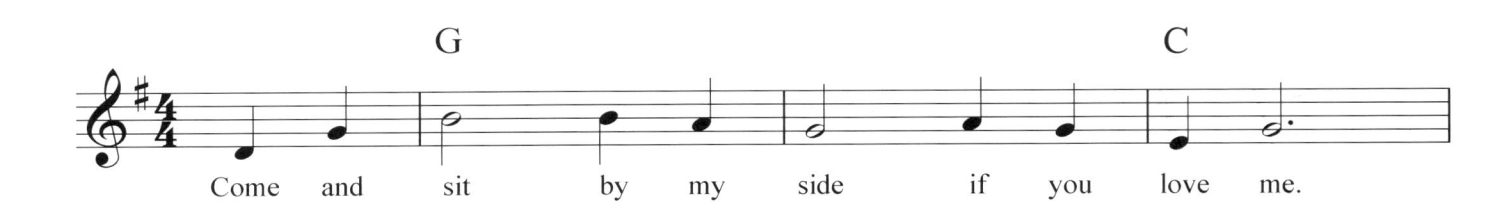

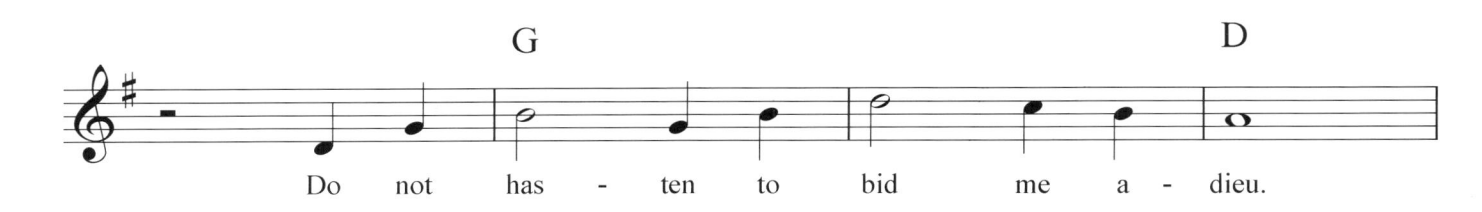

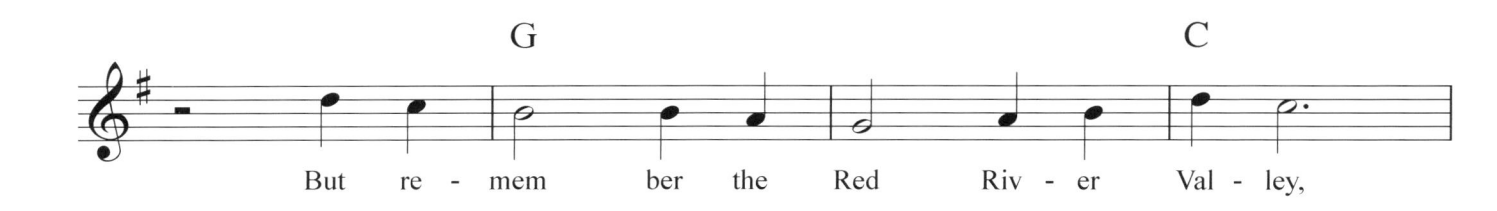

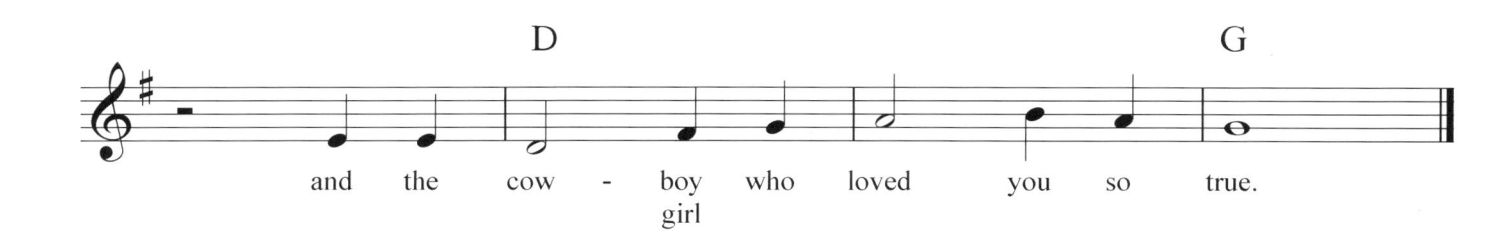

Strum Pattern

Come and sit by my side if you love me.

Do not has-ten to bid me a-dieu.

But re-mem-ber the Red Riv-er Val-ley,

and the cow-boy who loved you so true.
girl

© **Bradford Werner 2017, Victoria, BC, Canada**
Free & Premium Sheet Music & Tab: wernerguitareditions.com
Lessons, Pro Video, & Blog: thisisclassicalguitar.com

Full Chord Shapes

Memorize these chord shapes for the next few songs.

Notice the alternative fingering for the G chord. The first G chord is quite comfortable, the second is a bit of a stretch but easier to move to the C chord after. Choose one or have your teacher circle one for you.

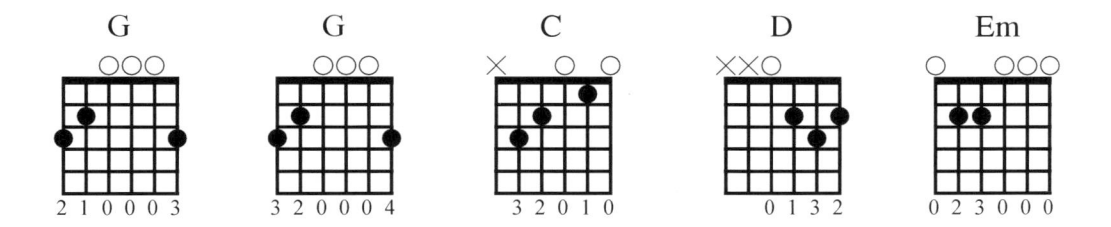

Tom Dooley - North Carolina Folk Song
Try out the G and C chords by strumming four beats per bar.

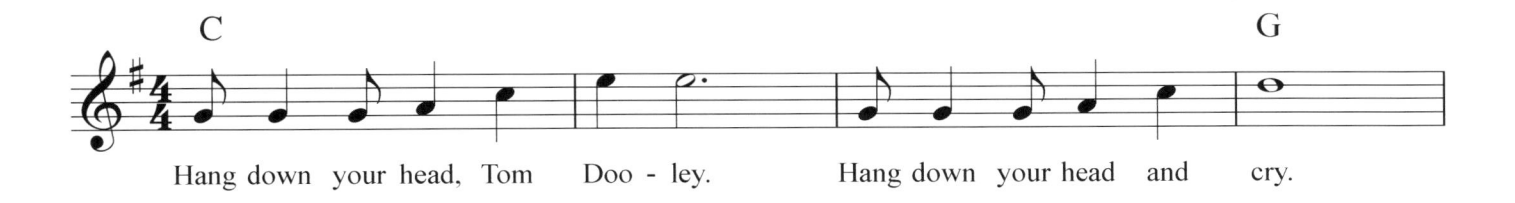

Hang down your head, Tom Doo - ley.   Hang down your head and cry.

Hang down your head, Tom Doo - ley.   Poor boy you're bound to die.

© Bradford Werner 2017, Victoria, BC, Canada
Free & Premium Sheet Music & Tab: wernerguitareditions.com
Lessons, Pro Video, & Blog: thisisclassicalguitar.com

Danny Boy

Traditional Irish

Bars containing two chords recieve two beats per chord.

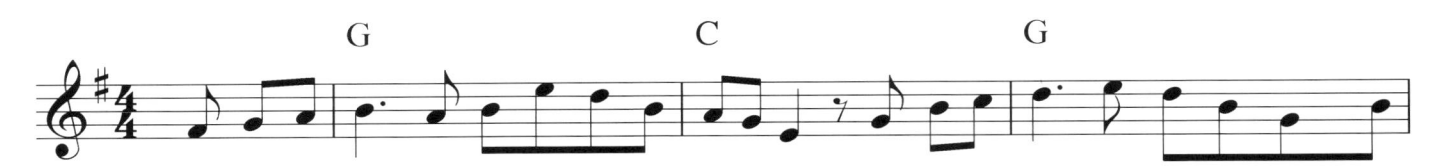

[G] Oh, Dan-ny boy, - the pipes the pipes are call-ing, [C] from glen to glen [G] and down the moun-tain

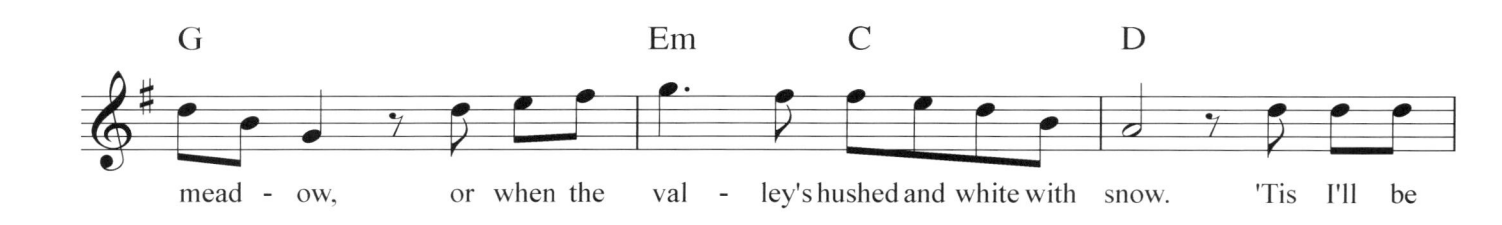

[D] side. The sum-mer's gone - [G] and all the ros-es fall-ing. [C] It's you, it's

[G] you, [D] must go, and I must bide. [G] But come ye back when sum-mer's in the [C]

[G] mead-ow, or when the [Em] val-ley's hushed [C] and white with snow. [D] 'Tis I'll be

[G] there in [C] sun-shine or in [G] shad-ow, oh, Dan-ny boy, [D] oh, Dan-ny boy, I love you [G] so!

Shenandoah

American Folksong

The chords change more often in this song.
Pick a slow tempo to begin.

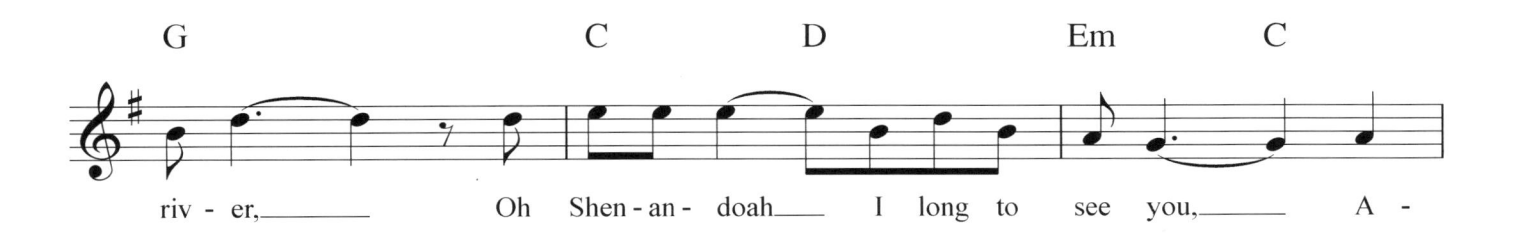

Oh. Shen-an-doah I long to see you, A - way you roll-ing riv-er, Oh Shen-an-doah I long to see you, A - way we're bound a - way a-cross the wide Miss-ou-ri.

© Bradford Werner 2017, Victoria, BC, Canada
Free & Premium Sheet Music & Tab: wernerguitareditions.com
Lessons, Pro Video, & Blog: thisisclassicalguitar.com

Scarborough Fair

Traditional

Strum with any strumming pattern as long as there are three beats per bar.
In the following pages we will also learn this song with fingerstyle accompaniment.

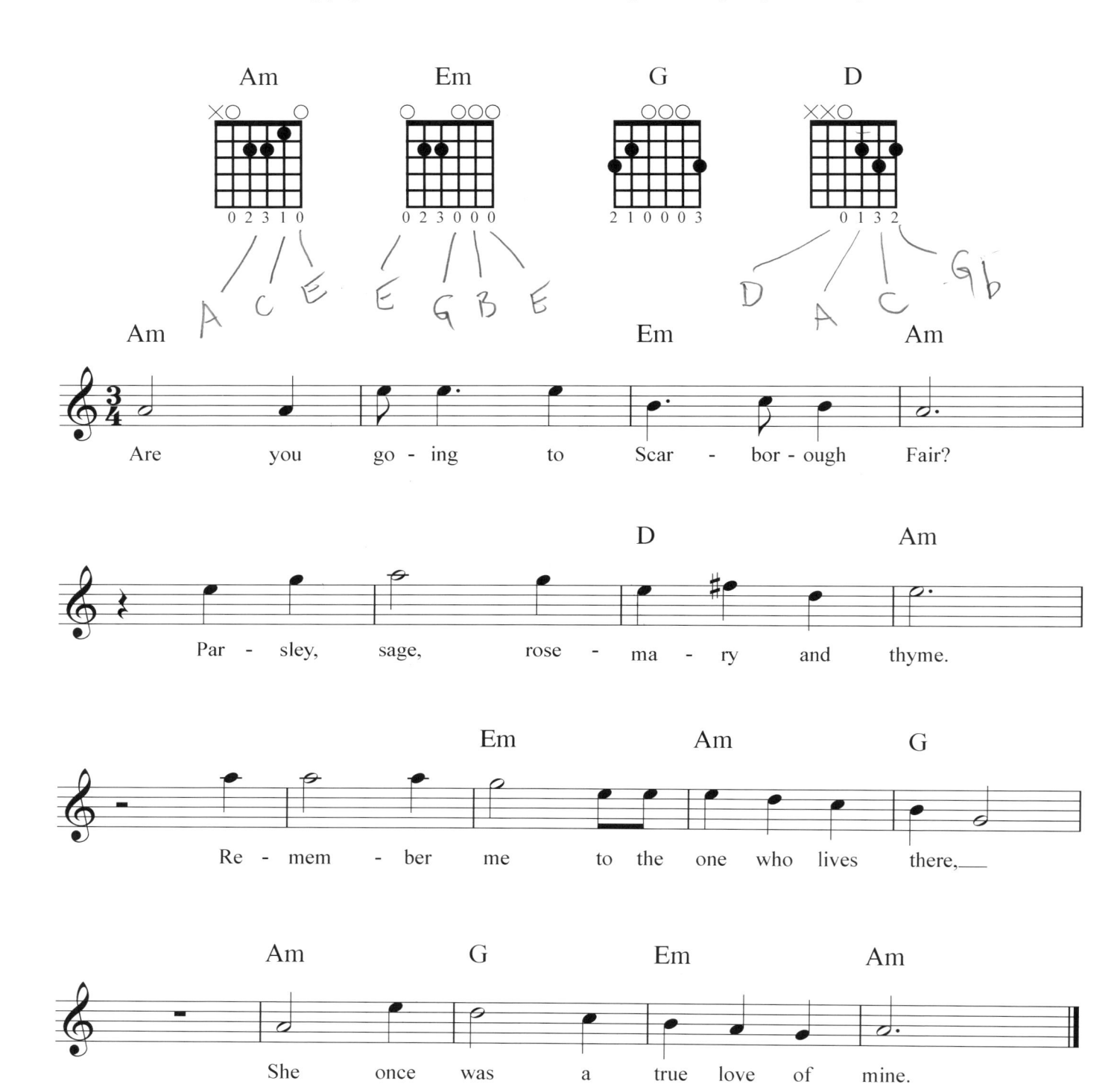

Am — A C E
Em — E G B E
G
D — D A C Gb

Am		Em	Am
Are you go-ing to	Scar - bor - ough	Fair?	

	D	Am
Par - sley, sage, rose - ma - ry and thyme.		

Em	Am	G
Re - mem - ber me to the one who lives there,___		

Am	G	Em	Am
She once was a true love of mine.			

© Bradford Werner 2017, Victoria, BC, Canada
Free & Premium Sheet Music & Tab: wernerguitareditions.com
Lessons, Pro Video, & Blog: thisisclassicalguitar.com

Tablature

Tablature (TAB) is another system of written music for guitar.
TAB is a visual representation of the six strings on the guitar.
The bottom line is the 6th string, the top line is the 1st string.
The numbers indicate the frets (not the fingering).

The below example demonstrates the same notes on both the notation staff and the TAB.

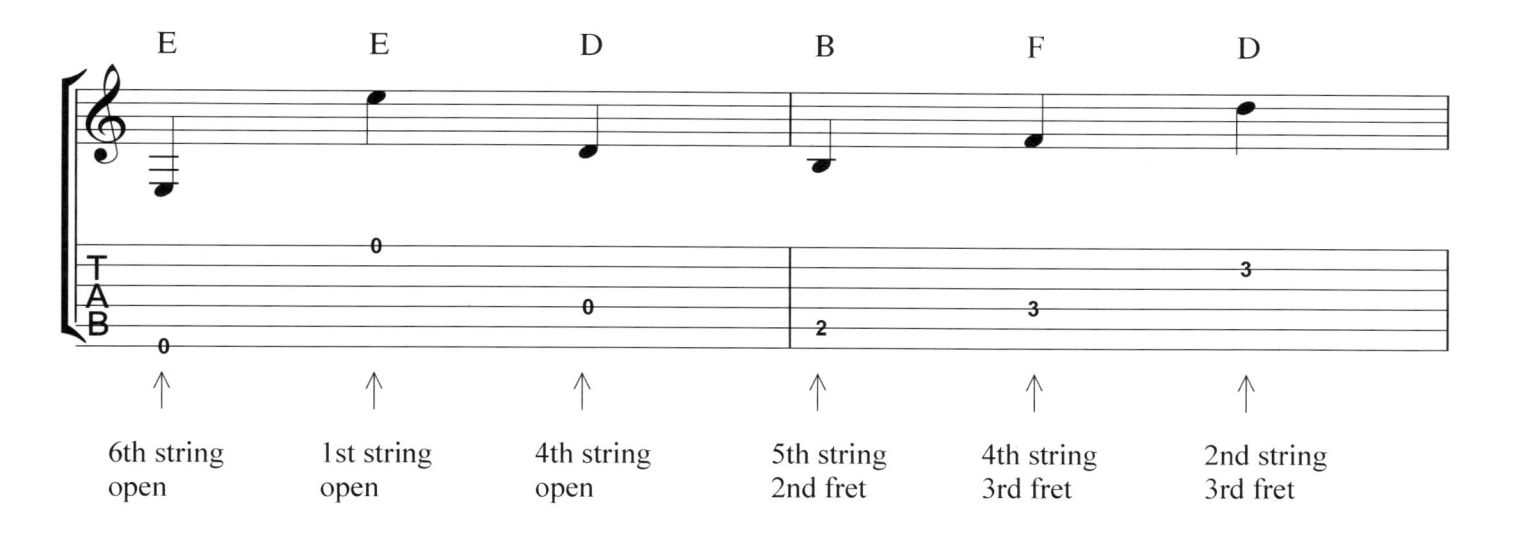

| 6th string | 1st string | 4th string | 5th string | 4th string | 2nd string |
| open | open | open | 2nd fret | 3rd fret | 3rd fret |

Please Note
Tablature has been in use for centuries going back to the Renaisance lute.
Modern TAB often omits rhythm and other musical indications so it has
some clear disadvantages. Most importantly, it does not allow you to
communicate with non-guitarists. However, it can still be useful for
direct guitar knowledge and popular music can often be found in TAB.

© Bradford Werner 2017, Victoria, BC, Canada
Free & Premium Sheet Music & Tab: wernerguitareditions.com
Lessons, Pro Video, & Blog: thisisclassicalguitar.com

Scarborough Fair (Fingerstyle)

Play the TAB as eighth notes (two notes for each beat).
When playing fingerstyle, only use the left hand fingers needed for each chord.
Let all notes sustain within each chord.

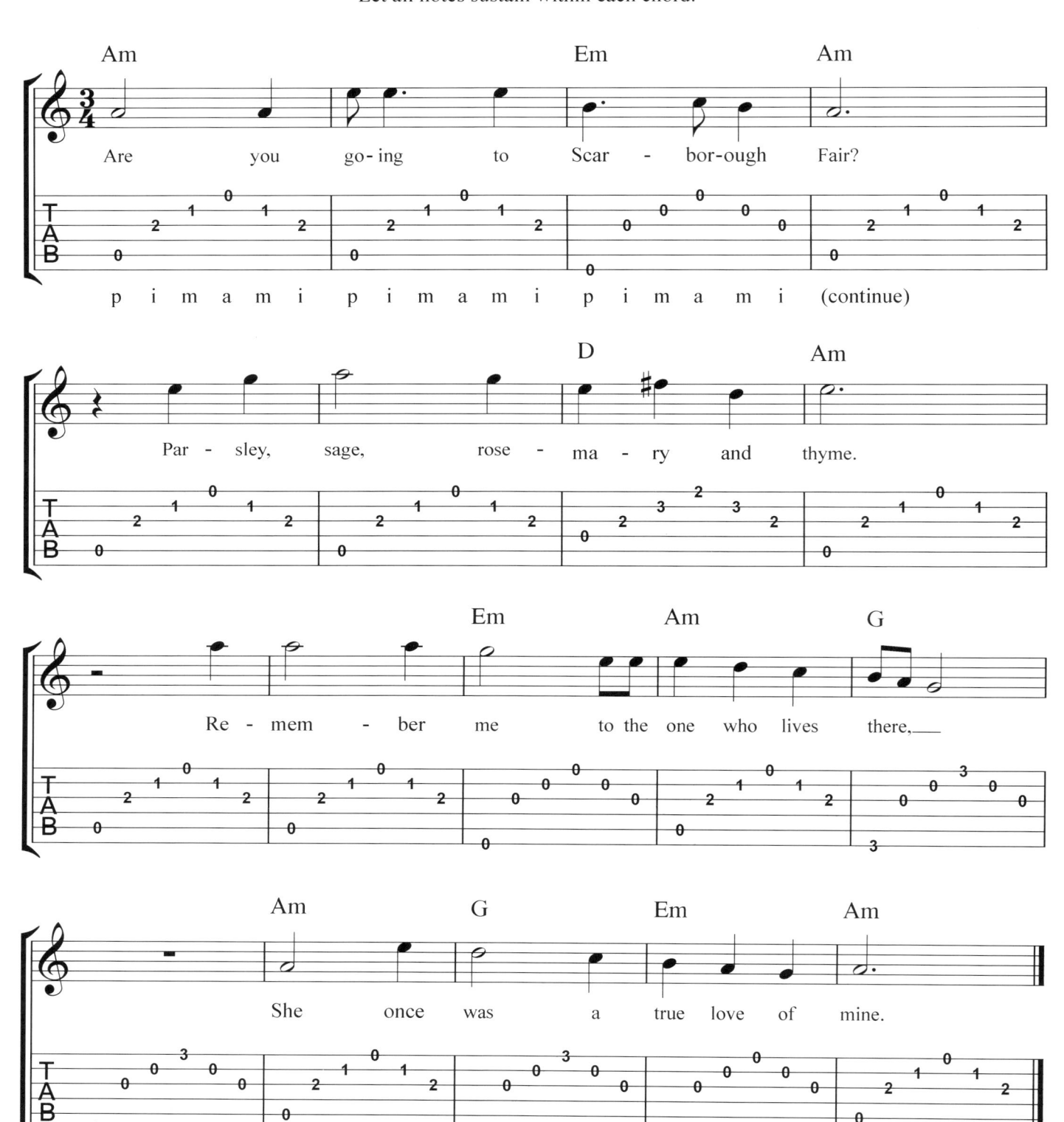

Are you go-ing to Scar-bor-ough Fair?
p i m a m i p i m a m i p i m a m i (continue)

Par-sley, sage, rose - ma - ry and thyme.

Re - mem - ber me to the one who lives there,

She once was a true love of mine.

© Bradford Werner 2017, Victoria, BC, Canada
Free & Premium Sheet Music & Tab: wernerguitareditions.com
Lessons, Pro Video, & Blog: thisisclassicalguitar.com

Will the Circle Be Unbroken?

Ada R. Habershon &
Charles H. Gabriel

The student plays the TAB (4 beats per bar).
Notice the bassline contained in this fingerstyle accompaniment.
Use your thumb for the bass notes and i, m, a for the top three strings.

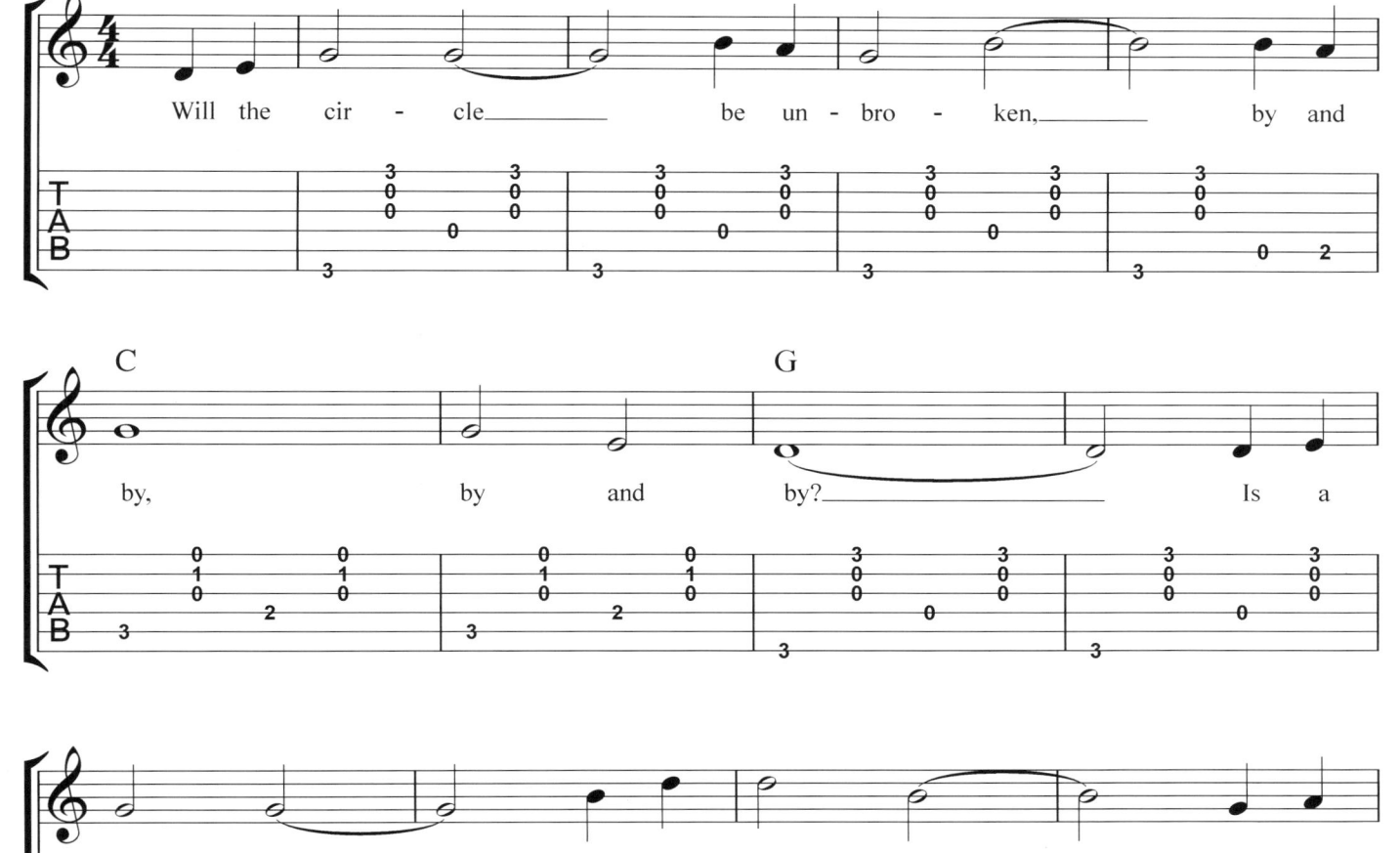

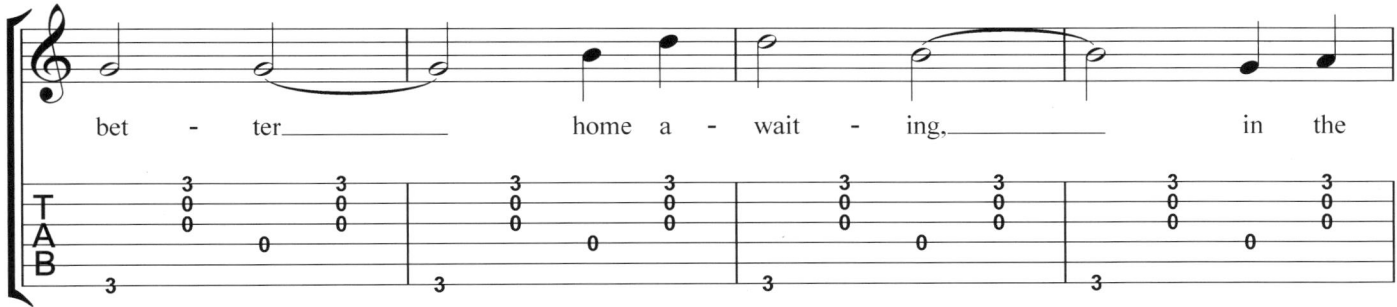

Lyrics: Will the cir - cle___ be un - bro - ken,___ by and by, by and by?___ Is a bet - ter___ home a - wait - ing,___ in the sky?___ in the sky?

© Bradford Werner 2017, Victoria, BC, Canada
Free & Premium Sheet Music & Tab: wernerguitareditions.com
Lessons, Pro Video, & Blog: thisisclassicalguitar.com

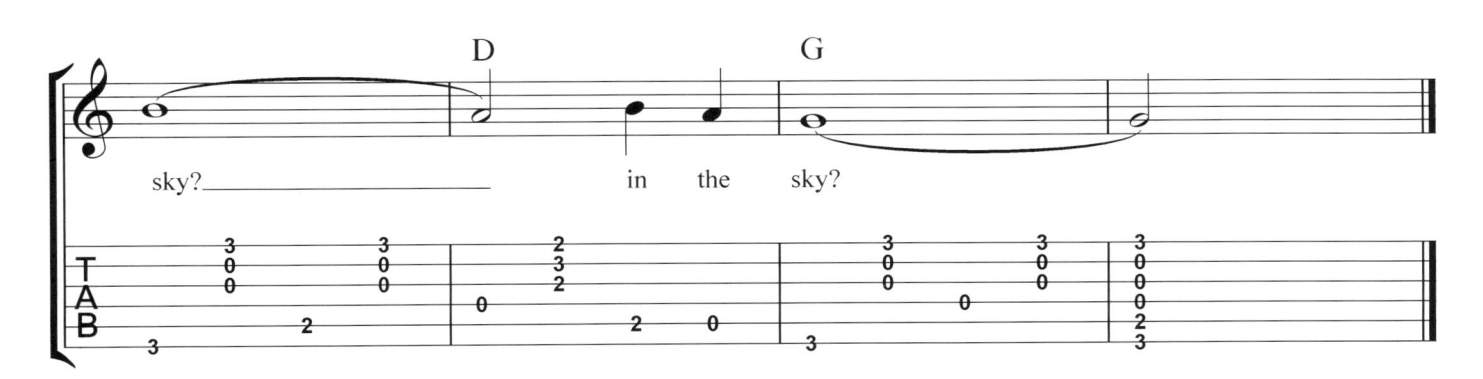

Saint James Infirmary Blues

American Folksong

The student should first strum the chords and then invent a simple fingerstyle accomapaniment.

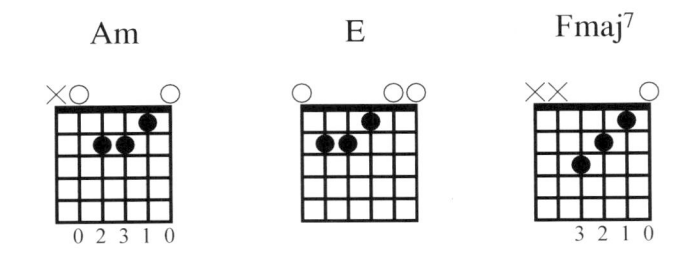

House of the Rising Sun

American Folksong

Strum the chords and then learn the TAB. Play the TAB as triplets (three notes to each beat) as indicted in the first bar.

Lyrics: There is a house in New Orleans they call the Rising Sun. It's been the ruin of many poor gal, and I oh Lord was one.

© Bradford Werner 2017, Victoria, BC, Canada
Free & Premium Sheet Music & Tab: wernerguitareditions.com
Lessons, Pro Video, & Blog: thisisclassicalguitar.com

Scales for Blues and Popular Music

Below is the pentatonic minor and blues scales up to the highest notes in position. These can be used for soloing over the following blues chords and other chord progressions such as House of the Rising Sun.

A Pentatonic Minor (open position)

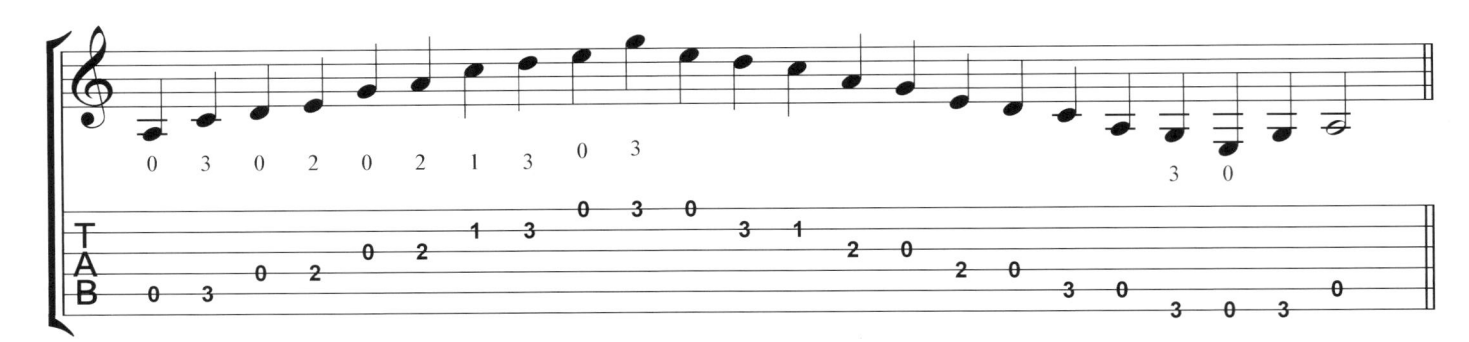

A Pentatonic Minor (closed position)

Closed position scales can be moved around the fingerboard to change the key.
Example: If you start the pattern on the 6th fret it will be an A# pentatonic minor scale.

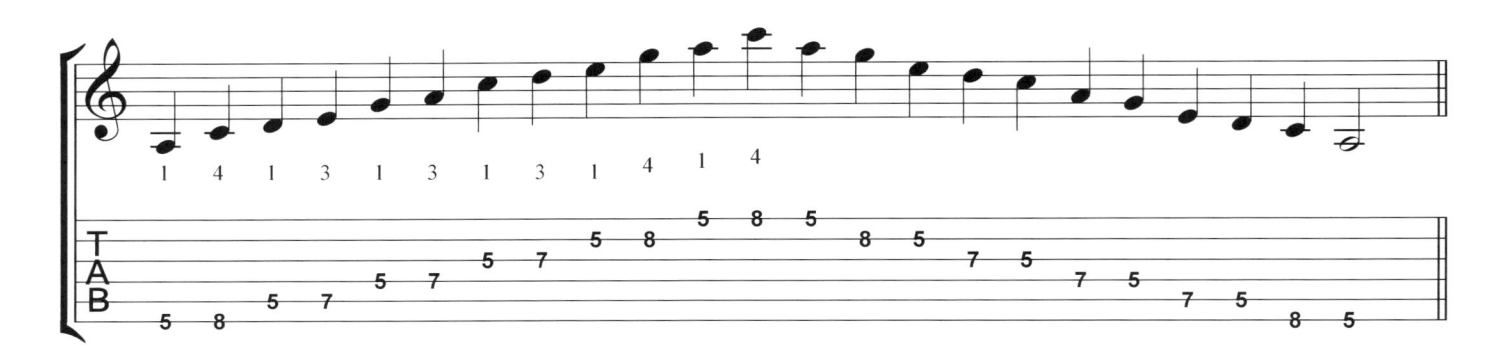

A Blues Scale (closed position)

By adding an extra note to the pentatonic minor scale we can create a blues scale.

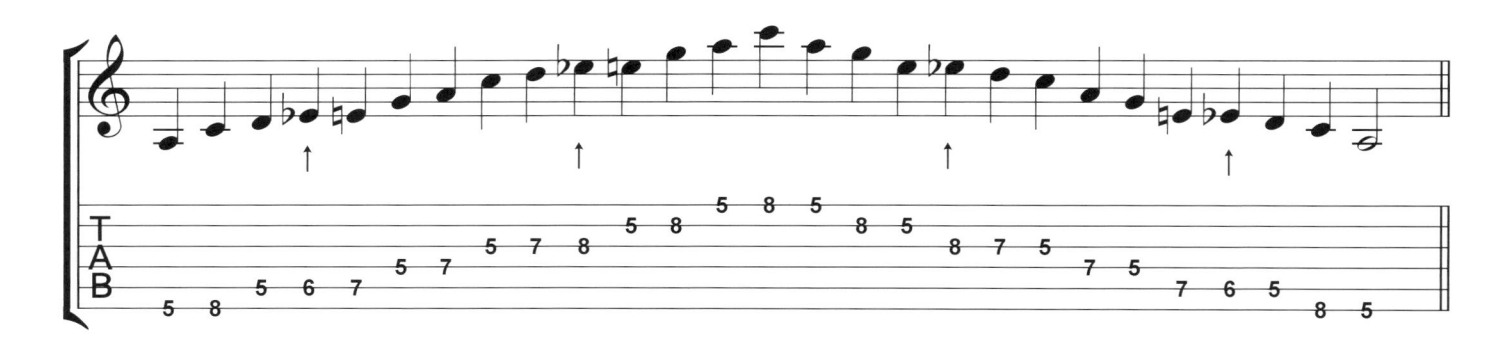

© Bradford Werner 2017, Victoria, BC, Canada
Free & Premium Sheet Music & Tab: wernerguitareditions.com
Lessons, Pro Video, & Blog: thisisclassicalguitar.com

Twelve Bar Blues

Use the TAB to check your note locations.
Take a solo using the A pentatonic minor scale.
When finished repeating, end using the A chord instead of E.
Swing the beat (think: long-short-long-short).

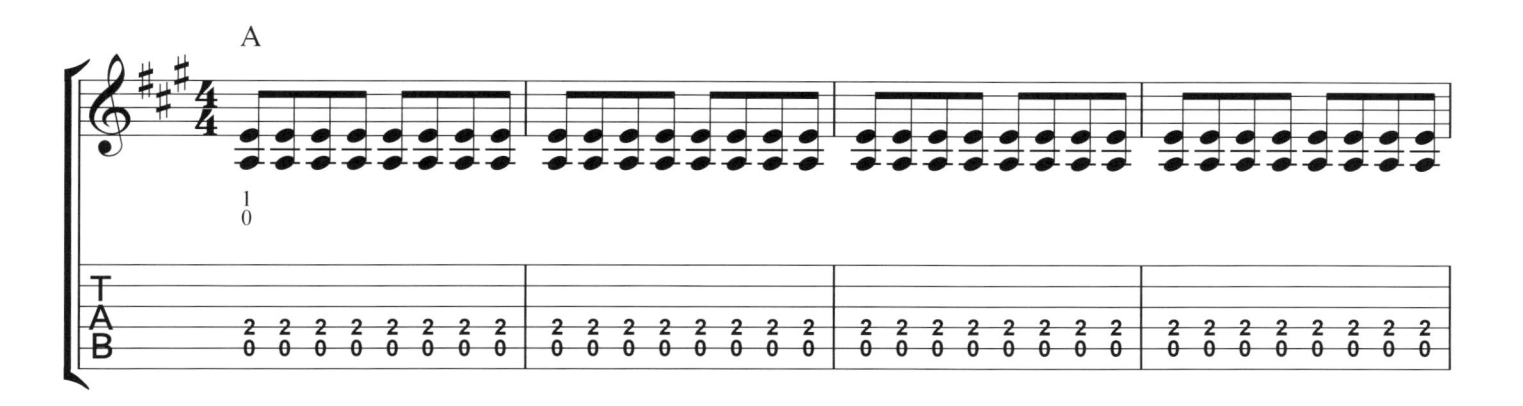

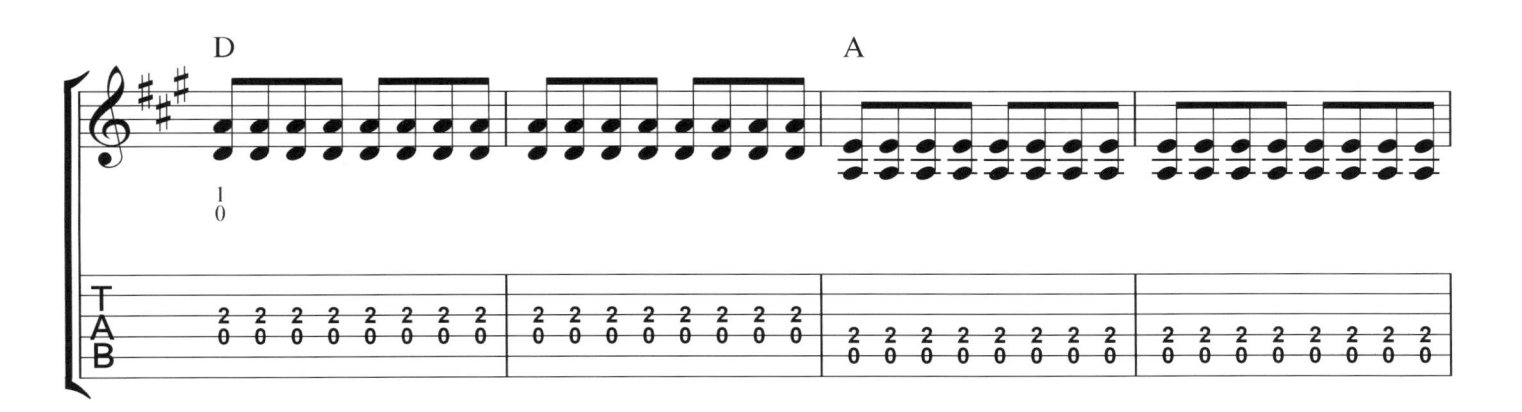

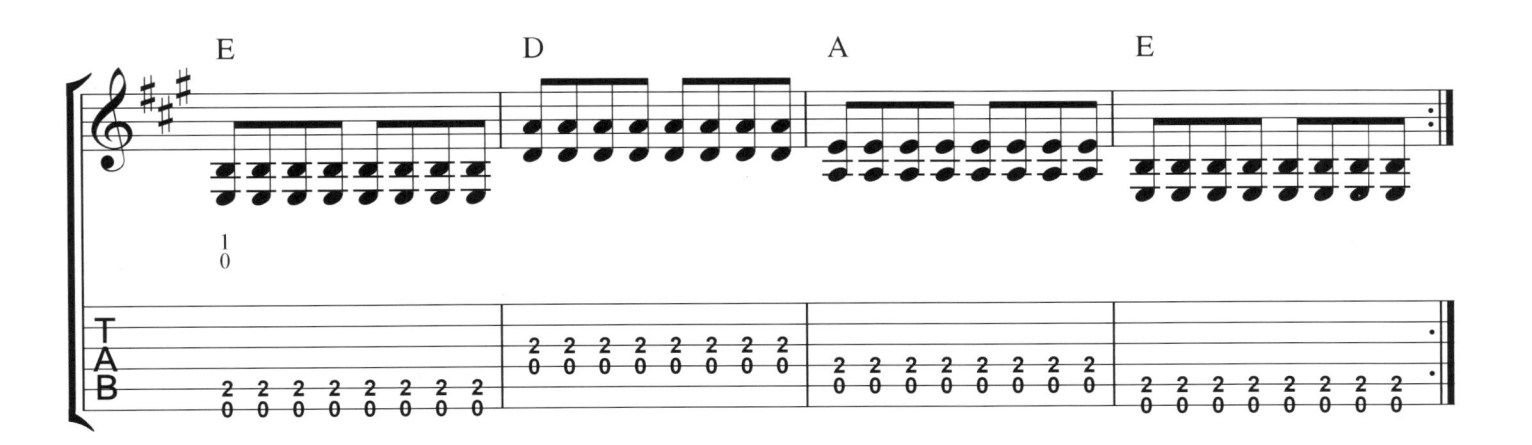

The Shuffle

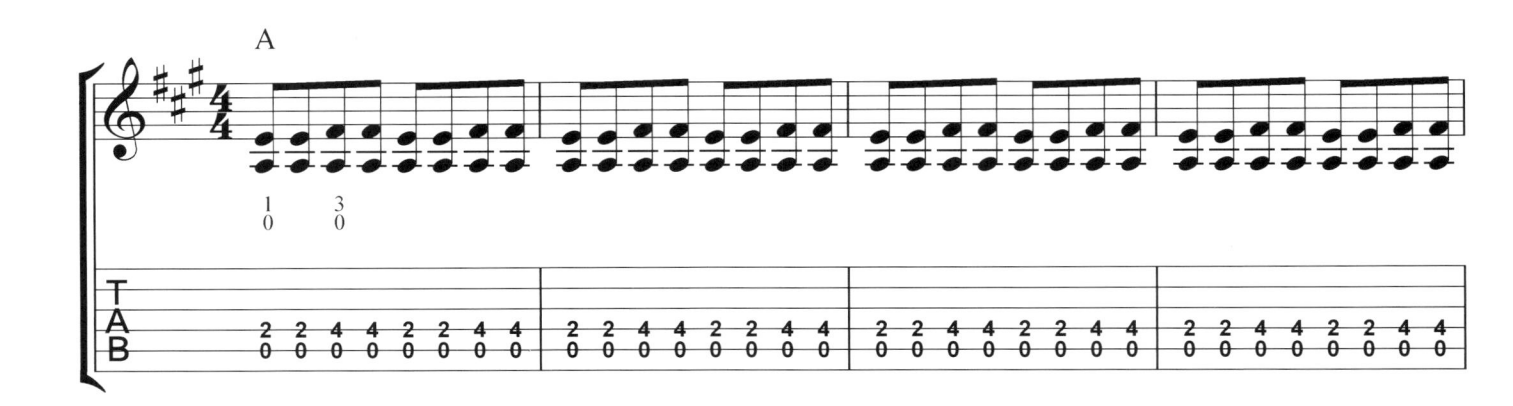

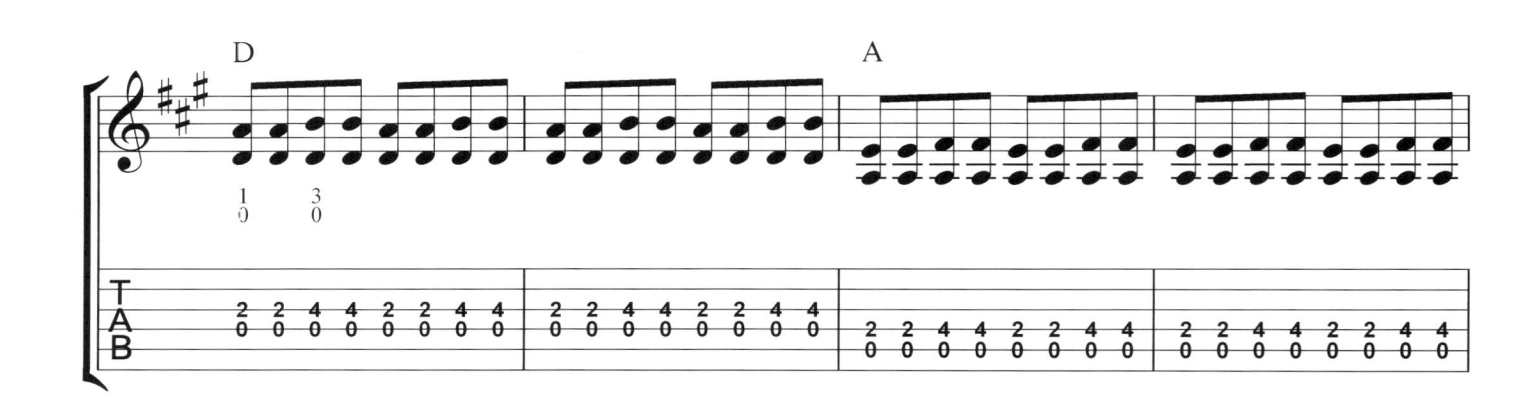

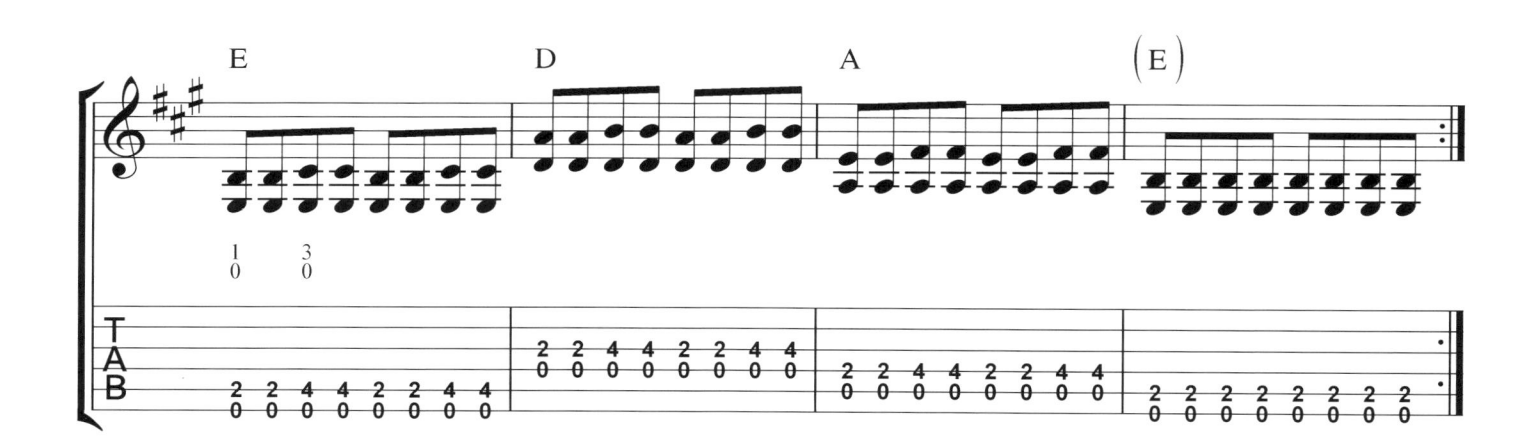

Rhythm Riff Blues

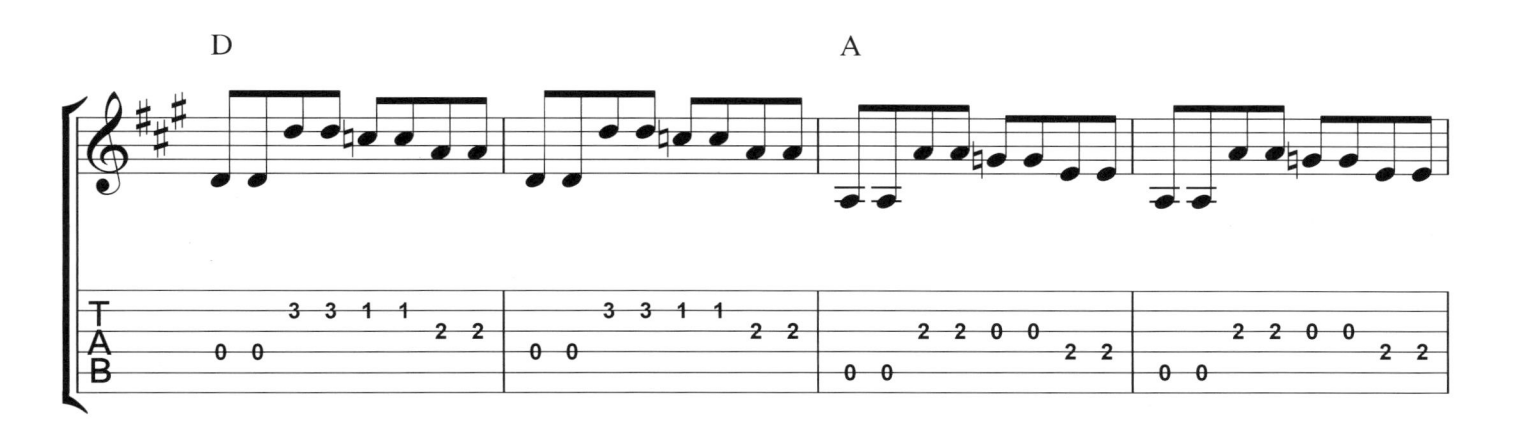

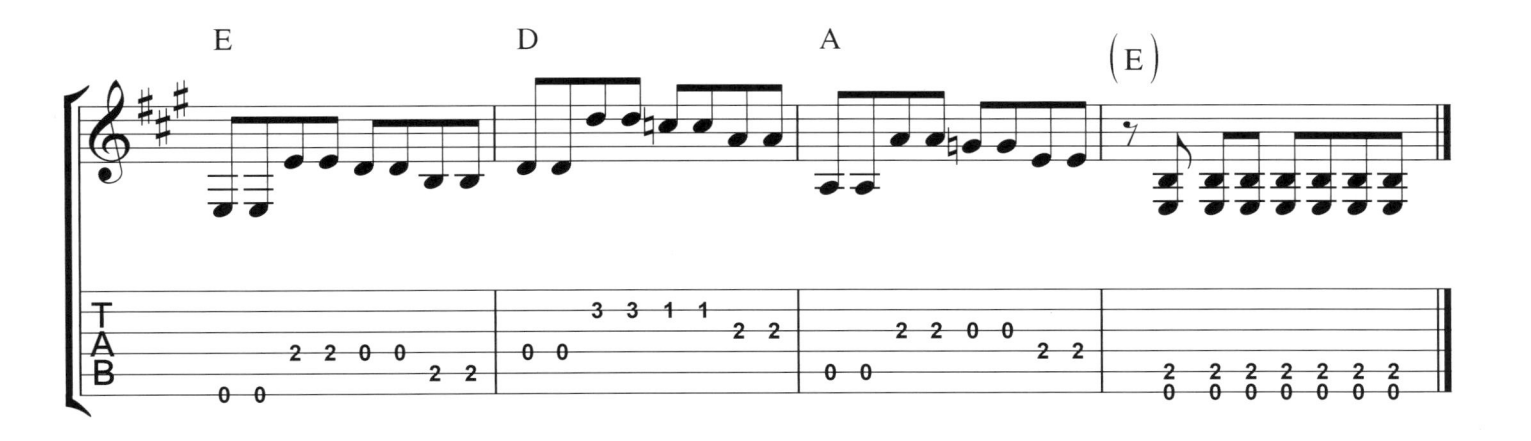

Right Hand Technique Exercises

No. 1 - i, m alternation in groups of four

No. 2 - i, m alternation in groups of three

No. 3 - p, i alternation
Remember to keep the thumb in front of the fingers during arpeggios. Checking your guitar position may help.

No. 4 - p, i, m arpeggio pattern

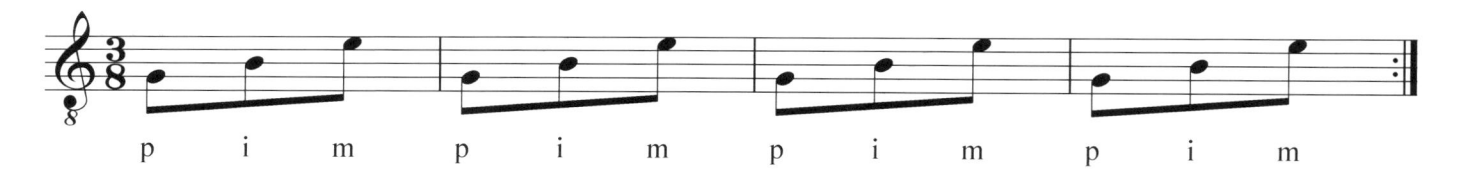

No. 5 - p, m, i arpeggio pattern

© **Bradford Werner 2017**, Victoria, BC, Canada
Free & Premium Sheet Music & Tab: wernerguitareditions.com
Lessons, Pro Video, & Blog: thisisclassicalguitar.com

No. 6 - p, i, m, a arpeggio pattern

No. 7 - p, a, m, i arpeggio pattern

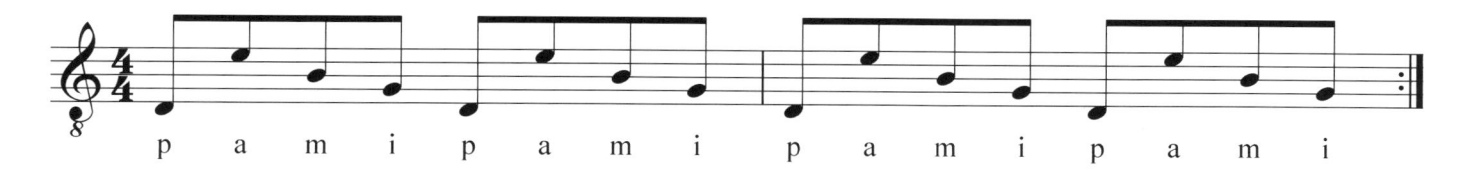

No. 8 - p, a, m, i arpeggio pattern

No. 9 - p, i, m, a arpeggio pattern

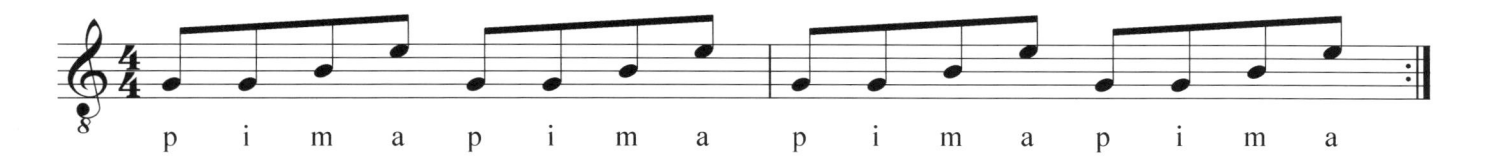

No. 10 - p, i, m, a bass strings arpeggio pattern

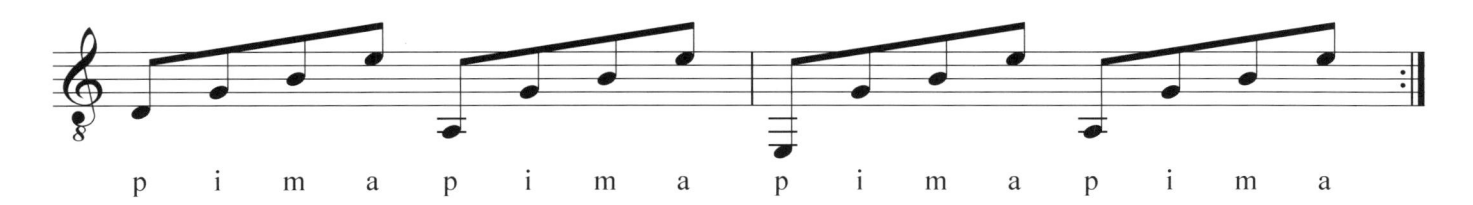

© **Bradford Werner 2017**, Victoria, BC, Canada

Free & Premium Sheet Music & Tab: wernerguitareditions.com
Lessons, Pro Video, & Blog: thisisclassicalguitar.com

Left Hand Technique Exercises

Tablature has been included to clarify the upper position playing.
A definition of tablature is given on page 81.

All of these exercises use a 'one-finger-per-fret' rule on a four fret group.
You can move these exercises to any four frets, lower frets increase the reach.

No. 1 - Two Finger Synchronization
Form a secure and legato synchronization between both hands.
Read the tablature as these exercises start on the 5th fret.

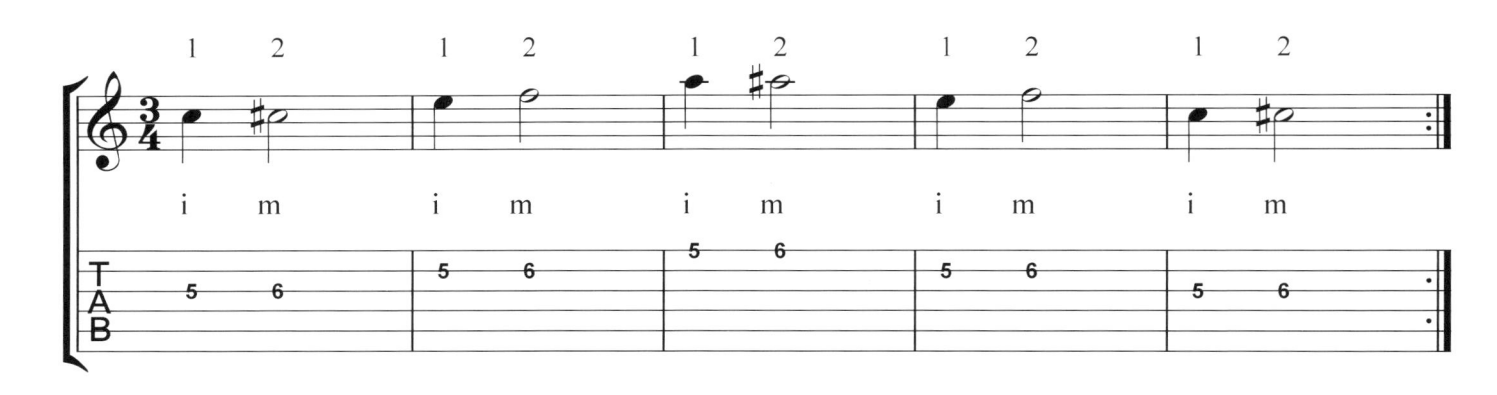

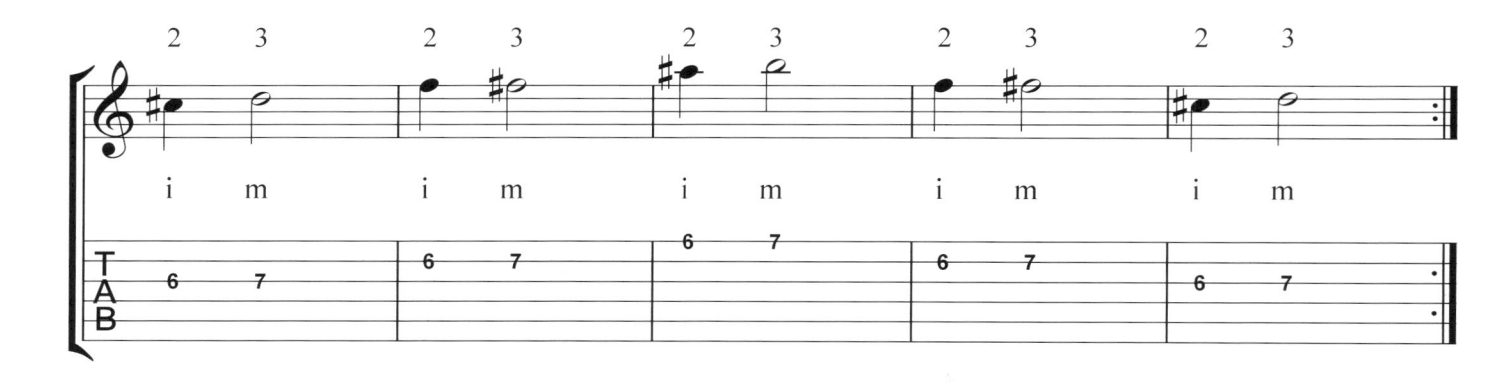

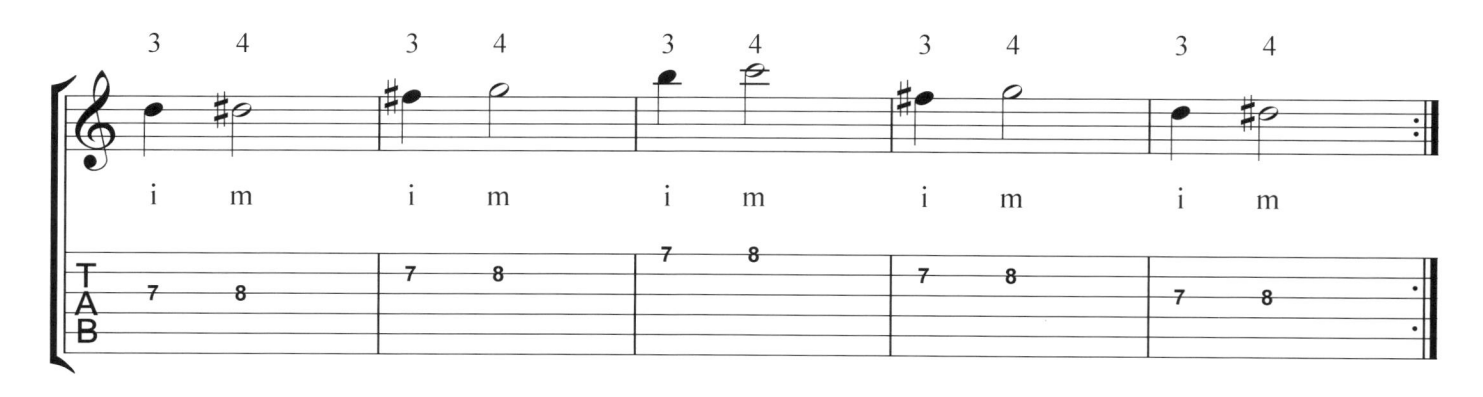

© Bradford Werner 2017, Victoria, BC, Canada
Free & Premium Sheet Music & Tab: wernerguitareditions.com
Lessons, Pro Video, & Blog: thisisclassicalguitar.com

No. 2 - Fingers 1-2-3-4 on all strings
Use your thumb for the three bass strings and i,m for the top three strings.

No. 4 - Fingers 1 and 4 on all strings
Keep the left hand aligned with the strings.

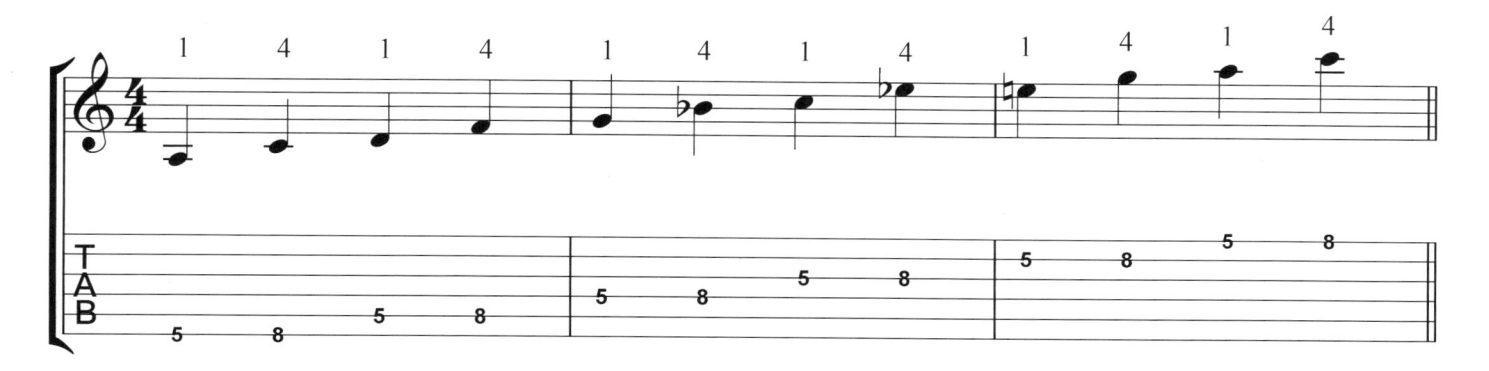

No. 3 - Fingers 1-2-3-4 with open strings
Continue this pattern down other strings. Students should be very careful to not overextend the left wrist.
Let all notes sustain, play on the fingertips with curved fingers, and avoid muting the open string.

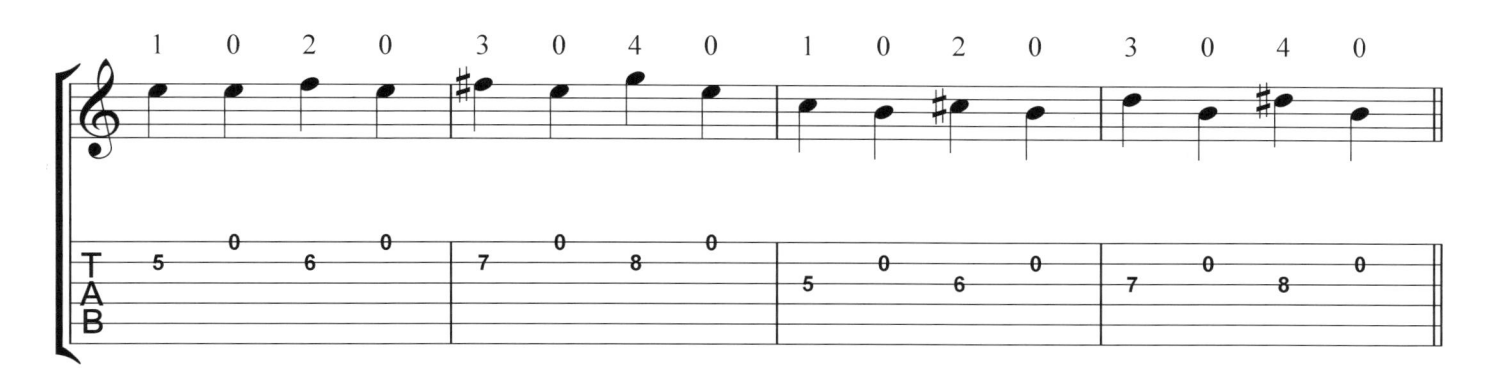

© Bradford Werner 2017, Victoria, BC, Canada
Free & Premium Sheet Music & Tab: wernerguitareditions.com
Lessons, Pro Video, & Blog: thisisclassicalguitar.com

Single String Chromatic Scales

These scales teach you the musical alphabet and every note on the guitar.
Memorize the pattern but don't worry about reading the notes.
The fingering is the same for all the strings. Say the note names out loud.
Upper position reading is covered in Volume Two.

1st String - E Chromatic

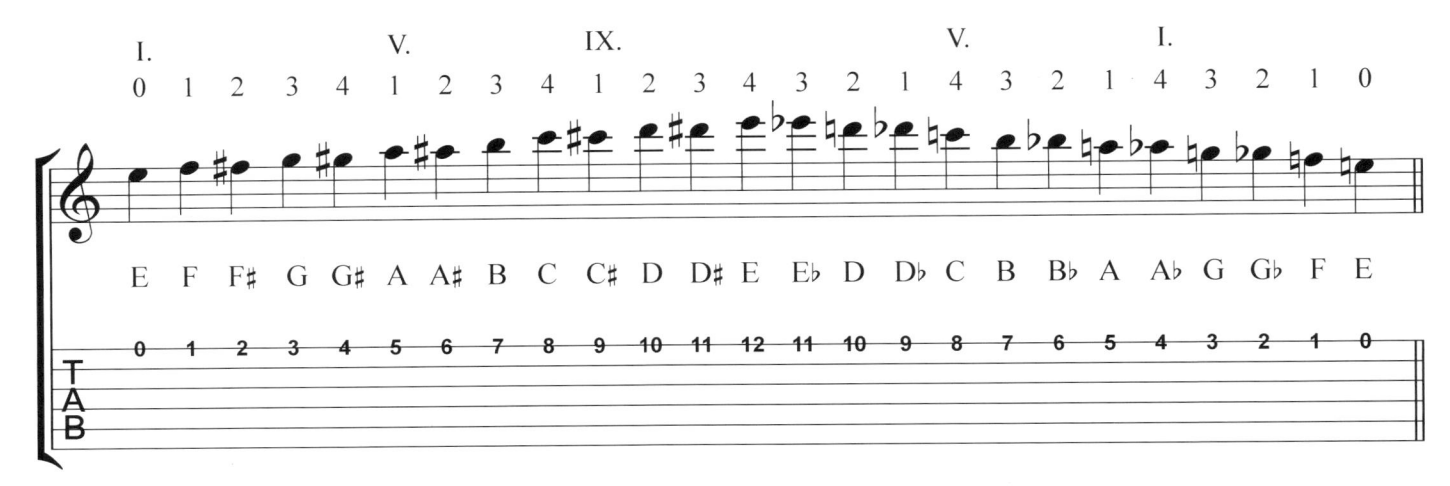

E F F# G G# A A# B C C# D D# E Eb D Db C B Bb A Ab G Gb F E

2nd String - B Chromatic

B C C# D D# E F F# G G# A A# B Bb A Ab G Gb F E Eb D Db C B

3rd String - G Chromatic

G G# A A# B C C# D D# E F F# G Gb F E Eb D Db C B Bb A Ab G

© Bradford Werner 2017, Victoria, BC, Canada
Free & Premium Sheet Music & Tab: wernerguitareditions.com
Lessons, Pro Video, & Blog: thisisclassicalguitar.com

4th String - D Chromatic

D D# E F F# G G# A A# B C C# D Db C B Bb A Ab G F# F E Eb D

TAB: 0 1 2 3 4 5 6 7 8 9 10 11 12 11 10 9 8 7 6 5 4 3 2 1 0

5th String - A Chromatic

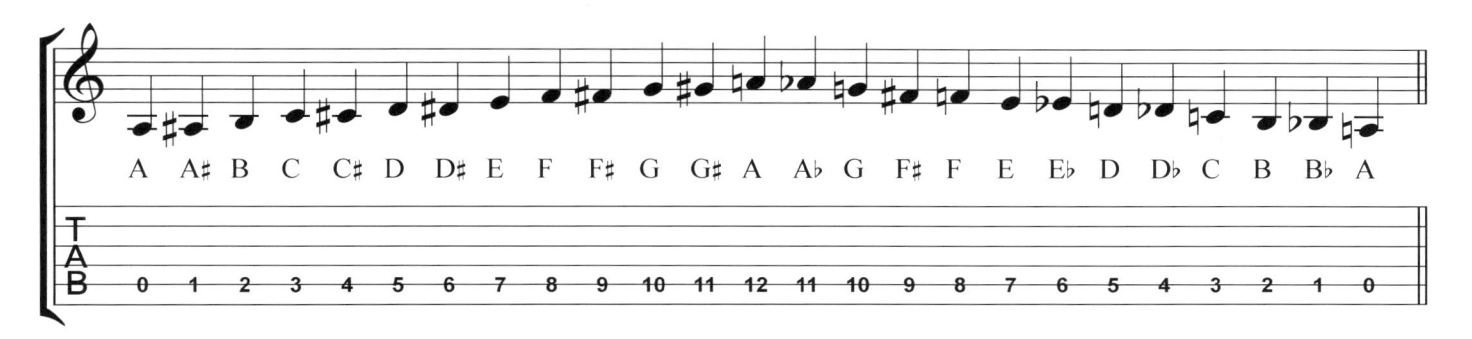

A A# B C C# D D# E F F# G G# A Ab G F# F E Eb D Db C B Bb A

TAB: 0 1 2 3 4 5 6 7 8 9 10 11 12 11 10 9 8 7 6 5 4 3 2 1 0

6th String - E Chromatic

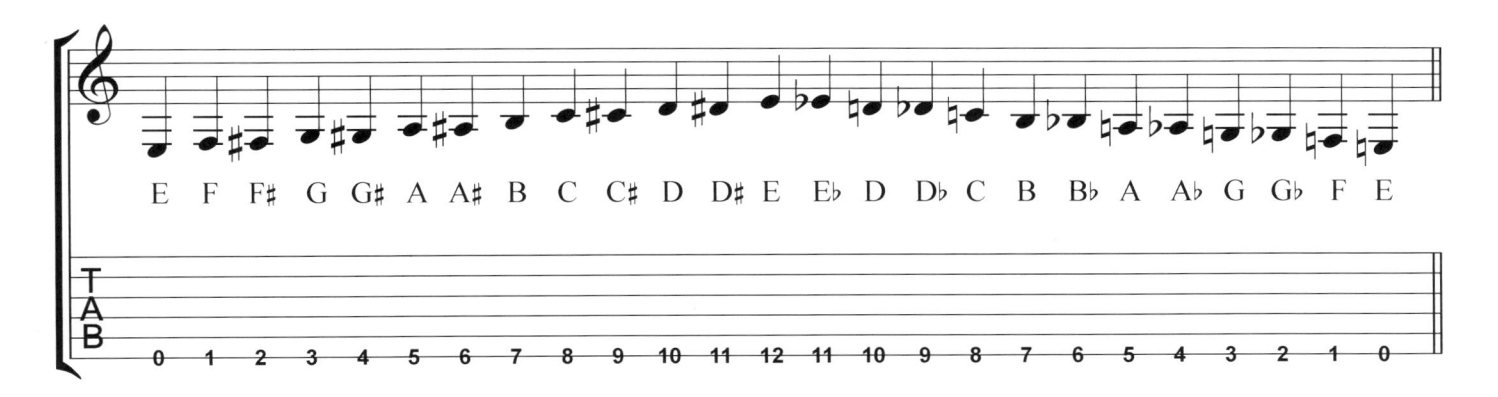

E F F# G G# A A# B C C# D D# E Eb D Db C B Bb A Ab G Gb F E

TAB: 0 1 2 3 4 5 6 7 8 9 10 11 12 11 10 9 8 7 6 5 4 3 2 1 0

© Bradford Werner 2017, Victoria, BC, Canada
Free & Premium Sheet Music & Tab: wernerguitareditions.com
Lessons, Pro Video, & Blog: thisisclassicalguitar.com

Scales

I have included a small number of scales in preparation for the next level of study. Beginners should continue to my Volume Two method book to fully understand the theory of scales, arpeggios, and key signatures, as well as practice approaches.

E Chromatic 1 Octave

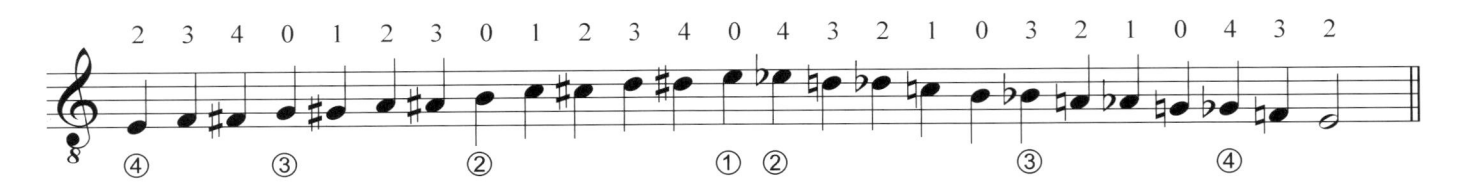

E Chromatic 2 Octaves

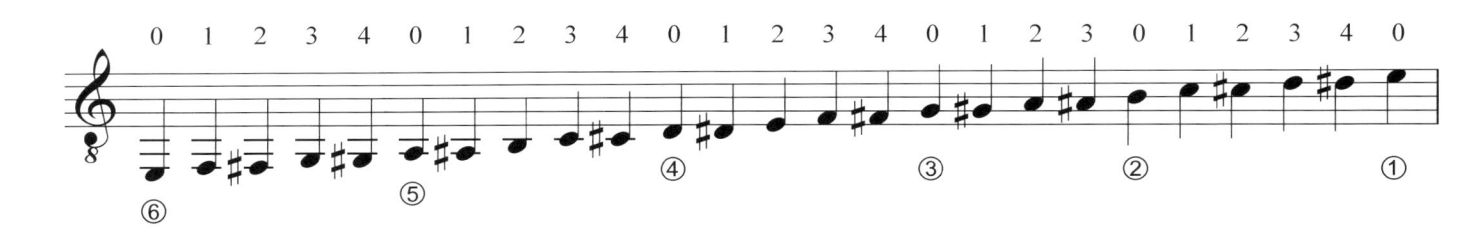

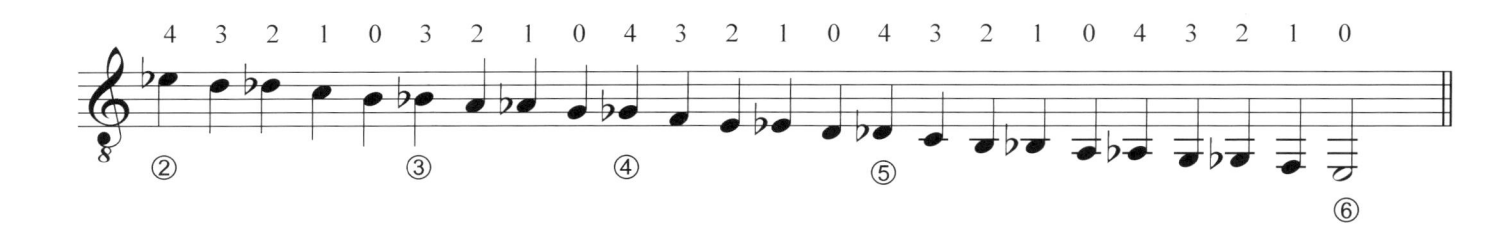

One Octave Major Scales

These scales have been left unfingered for flexiblity in teaching styles.
Key Signatures will be discussed in my Volume Two method book.
I have added accidentals in addition to the key signature.

C Major

G Major Upper Octave

G Major Lower Octave

F Major

© Bradford Werner 2017, Victoria, BC, Canada
Free & Premium Sheet Music & Tab: wernerguitareditions.com
Lessons, Pro Video, & Blog: thisisclassicalguitar.com

A Natural Minor

E Natural Minor

D Natural Minor